A DISTINCTIVELY
BAPTIST CHURCH

Smyth & Helwys Publishing, Inc.
6316 Peake Road
Macon, Georgia 31210-3960
1-800-747-3016
©2008 by Smyth & Helwys Publishing

Library of Congress Cataloging-in-Publication Data

Prevost, Ronnie, 1949–
A Distinctively Baptist Church / by Ronnie Prevost.
p. cm.
ISBN 978-1-57312-502-4
1. Baptists. I. Title.

BX6331.3P74 2008
286—dc22
2007045032

A DISTINCTIVELY BAPTIST CHURCH

RENEWING YOUR CHURCH IN PRACTICE

Ronnie Prevost

Dedication

To Tom and David, my Baptist brothers in every sense of the term.
To my brother and sister Baptists of the St. Vincent & the Grenadines
Baptist Convention on the thirtieth anniversary of their founding.
To my beloved colleagues of the Logsdon School of Theology, *real* Baptists
with whom I have been privileged to walk and work.
Most of all—to God, in deepest gratitude for salvation
and the rich Baptist heritage I have enjoyed.

Contents

Introduction

The first purpose of this introduction is actually to make two introductions: one to the book and its design and purposes, the other to its writer (me). One other purpose is to offer you, the reader, several words of caution. Even if you choose to skip the two earlier parts of this introduction, please do not overlook the latter.

If you are reading this book, you are probably a Baptist. After all, who else would be interested in becoming or in leading their church to be a distinctively Baptist church? And if you are attracted to this topic, this may not be the first book you have seen and/or read about Baptists, their theology, and their practice. Many have been written—especially recently.

So why this one? The answer is simple. Though much has been written about what Baptists believe or have believed, there seem to be three unfortunate gaps. First, most of these books seem to be aimed at clergy and theological scholars and not at laity. Second, little has been said or written about how certain key historically Baptist beliefs should shape the way a church looks and functions. Third, there is a lack of material designed to help churches work through how their Baptist heritage should and will shape their life and witness.

This book and its free downloadable teaching guide (available at www.helwys.com/prevost_tg.pdf) intend to fill those three voids. Through them, we will first explore the foundations: Baptist history and doctrine. These may sound like "dry" topics at first. However, many people who research their genealogy and heritage find—often to their surprise—that the work is fresh and exciting. (My hope and prayer is that you and your church will make the same discovery.)

Then we will ask ourselves, so what? You see, even if we are excited by our Baptist heritage, it matters little if we do not live and show it in our churches. Toward this end we will ask ourselves how Baptist doctrine can and should influence our worship, evangelism, missions, and education ministries as Baptist churches. Through the study and reflection questions, you will be challenged to consider how you and your church *can* and *will* live out your wonderful Baptist heritage right where you are. That is *your* decision. You and your church are independent and autonomous under the Lordship of Jesus Christ.

You are probably also (rightfully) asking yourself about me. Why, beyond the above, am I writing this? First and foremost, it is because of who

I am—a Baptist. Reared by Baptist parents. Saved and baptized at the age of seven in Colonial Baptist Church in Memphis, Tennessee. Called to ministry at the age of nine at a Royal Ambassadors Camp at Harding Lake, Alaska. Grew up going to Sunday schools and Vacation Bible Schools in Baptist churches in Tennessee, Alaska, Washington, and Mississippi (I was an Army brat). Received degrees from two Baptist schools. Licensed and ordained to the ministry by Baptist churches. Ordained a deacon by a Baptist church. Served as minister and deacon in Baptist churches since 1968. Taught in three Baptist colleges and universities and three Baptist seminaries. Written Bible study and missions education curricula for four Baptist publishing houses. Baptists such as John Smyth, Roger Williams, and E. Y. Mullins were among my boyhood heroes (and they remain so).

Being Baptist is almost all I know. Being Baptist *is* all I know how to be in my Christian walk and call. It matters so much that it is one of my primary areas of research. It is one of the subjects I teach.

Being Baptist matters to me. I find it disturbing that so many Baptists today have forgotten what it means—beyond the mode of baptism—to *be* Baptist. They have forgotten their heritage. Countless Baptist forebears bought and wrote that heritage with their blood. We may remember the names of some. We may have forgotten some. We will never know the names of many. We Baptists today owe them. It is not so much whether or not we remember and honor their names. What is important is whether we honor the legacy they left us.

Some suggest that we are in a "post-denominational age." They say that church people today are more concerned with being *Christian* rather than being *Baptist*. Me, too. Being in Christ is more important than *anything*.

However, being Christian does not mean that every other bit of our identity is lost. For many of us, the Baptist way of being Christian is a unique heritage. I may be naïve, but I think that people today are hungering for more than a name. They crave something in which to believe. Something beyond themselves. Something that matters. My challenge to you through this book is that you become—and lead your church to become—Baptist not only in name, but in truth.

Now, here are the words of caution I mentioned in the opening paragraph. Firstly, I cannot and do not claim to speak for all Baptists of any era. Not of the past. Certainly not of the present. What I share is from my own study and research. It is not an exhaustive and comprehensive history. That was and is not my intention. Nor do I think that is what churches want and need.

Secondly, I am just one Baptist. Some other Baptist could take this same outline and write a book with different conclusions. That is fine, because that, too, is part of what it means to be a Baptist. Similarly, you may shape your and your church's being Baptist in a way that varies from mine.

Thirdly, the mainstream of my own Baptist heritage is that which I am addressing. As you will see in the first chapter, there are today many kinds of Baptists. Most have some common roots. There are also a vast number of differences in their respective histories. The historical focus here will be on Baptists of the American South and how they grew out of the English Baptists.

Finally, Baptists *are* going to disagree on matters of doctrine and practice. More so on some, less on others. Not even the apostles Peter and Paul agreed on everything! Do not let your discussion, dialogue, and shaping become an exercise by which you exclude those who disagree. Rather, use it as an opportunity to learn from and understand our heritage *and* each other. (In such a diverse world, this can be a wonderful witness to God's redeeming power!) Clarifying and living out who you are does not mean you cannot cooperate with those who differ. For example, being distinctively Baptist does not mean that one should not, cannot, or does not work alongside others, be they Protestant, Catholic, Jewish, or whatever.

The issue is finding a balance. That is a tricky proposition. My best guess is that the answer is rooted in love and respect.

Therefore, as we enter into our study together, let us keep before us the instruction my mother always gave me: "Be nice." More importantly, we *must* consider and abide by what we read in 1 John 4:7-21 and 1 Corinthians 13. In fact, why not—right now—put down this book. Before you pick it up again and continue, read those two passages. Pray over them. Let God's Holy Spirit speak to you 2hrough them and prepare your spirit, mind, and heart.

Chapter 1

A Brief Introduction to Baptist History: Where Did We Come From?

Where did we Baptists come from? What are our roots? I have heard that a tree has as many roots beneath the ground as it has branches above. That is a pretty good picture for our "Baptist Family Tree." First, there are many different kinds of Baptists in North America. As recently as 1995, one book listed twenty different Baptist groups in the United States alone.[1]

Then there are Baptists around the world. For example, the Moscow Theological Seminary in Russia is owned and operated by a denomination called the Russian-Ukrainian Union of Evangelical Christians-Baptists. On the Web site of the Baptist World Alliance (http://www.bwanet.org), General Secretary Dr. Denton Lotz put it this way: "The Baptist World Alliance is a unique fellowship of a community of 80 million Baptists in more than 214 conventions worldwide. This in itself shows how we represent a broad constituency of believers from Argentina to Zimbabwe from Albania to New Zealand, from Japan to the Ukraine!"

Now that is a lot of Baptists from many different—and differing—groups, denominations, countries. Not all of them agree on various doctrines. Not all of them have exactly the same family tree. You see, we Baptists have many different roots. In this short chapter and book we cannot deal with all of them—certainly not in any depth. However, to sort them out and try to make some sense out of this maze, we will examine Baptist history from two viewpoints: Baptists in Europe and then Baptists in the Americas.

Of course, it is not unusual to study back through history and learn about people and groups with some beliefs that Baptists would later hold. But that does not necessarily make them authentically "Baptist." They may have held some very non-Baptist beliefs also. Nevertheless, many of them contributed to the flow of history that fed into or became the Baptist movement. So it is important that we consider some of these groups.

But first, let's remember that the Christian church existed long before Baptists arose. In fact, most groups rise in response or reaction to the way things are—the *status quo*. The same is true of Baptists. Let us start by condensing pre-Baptist Christian history into just a few paragraphs so we can understand the world to which Baptists were responding.

The Pre-Baptist Christian Church and World

Persecution of the Early Church

Early in the New Testament book of Acts we read of Jesus' ascension. Soon after, there happened the wondrous events at Pentecost: the coming of the Holy Spirit and the conversion of thousands. Following these, various parties of the Jews began to persecute the disciples and other followers of Jesus. The Sadducees, who did not believe in resurrection, denied that Jesus even *could* have risen from the dead. The Pharisees rejected the idea that Jesus was the Messiah, much less the very Son of God. The Sanhedrin commanded Peter and the other disciples not to preach their message, the gospel. Peter responded, in Acts 5:29, "We must obey God rather than men" (NASB). Not surprisingly, the persecution continued. Acts 7 records the Sanhedrin's stoning of Stephen. Stephen had been among the first group of church leaders (many call these seven men the first deacons) selected by the church (Acts 6). The account of Stephen's death is the first reference to the young man Saul who would become the great missionary/evangelist Paul and who would face much persecution himself.

At first, the Roman Empire ignored Christianity. The Romans saw Christians as more or less simply another group of Jews. It was not long before that changed. The Roman Empire first began to worship the "spirit of Rome." That evolved into emperor-worship. The result was that those living in the Roman Empire were expected to declare, "Caesar is lord." Christians, who recognized only Jesus as Lord, refused. At this, the Romans called them "atheists." Further, there were widespread misunderstandings of what Christians taught and how they lived and worshipped. For example, the Lord's Supper was considered cannibalism. These false impressions resulted in Christianity being outlawed in and of itself. The persecution took many forms, such as imprisonment, execution, and economic oppression, to name a few.

Heresy in the Early Church

Not only was the early church being attacked from the outside by persecution, but attack also came from within by false teaching. Often, this arose from previously existing religions and philosophies. Sometimes, Christian converts would bring with them some of their previous beliefs, practices, and worldviews. For example, we know there was one group known as the Gnostics. Simply stated, they believed everything fleshly was evil and everything spiritual was good. They believed the fleshly and the spiritual could not mix. So, they concluded, Jesus could not have been both God and man. Rather, they concluded, Jesus only *appeared* to be flesh. Still others believed Jesus to have been either created or, at least, spiritually inferior to God.

The danger of these and other heresies is that those who believed them could easily adopt and adapt the words of Christianity and even claim that label for themselves. God inspired many of the books of the New Testament to be written in response to false teaching. John wrote his Gospel and 1 John, among other reasons, to combat Gnosticism. One can read 1 John 1:1 and see John's point that he had *touched* Jesus—proof that Jesus had indeed been there "in the flesh." Paul wrote his letter to the Colossians to show that Jesus was not created, but was fully God.

The Early Church Responds

The early church did not ignore either persecution or heresy. As we can see, one way the church responded to heresies was through writings that explained correct doctrine. There were many other Christian writings, however. Some are described as "apologies." That does not mean the authors were sorry for being Christians. Rather, apologies in this sense were written (often to Roman officials!) to explain Christian practices and beliefs. Other early Christian writings were intended to teach correct doctrine and practices to other Christians.

The early church also developed brief statements of faith. The statement "Jesus is Lord" (in Romans 10:9 and 1 Corinthians 12:3) may have been one. The confessions were simple and easily memorized. Because so many of the early Christians were illiterate, this was important and helpful.

One might ask, "Okay, who was producing these Christian writings and confessions?" Simply stated, they were the Christian leaders who stepped up in the wake of the Apostles. The New Testament mentions various church offices: pastors, deacons, elders, etc. Who they were and how they were to function is not always clear. For example, the Greek word we often understand to mean "pastor" is *episkopos*, which means "overseer." *Diakonos* is the Greek word from which we get the term "deacon," but it simply means "servant." Likewise, the Greek *presbuteros* means "elder." Sometimes it seems to refer simply to an older person. Sometimes its use indicates a church office. Several New Testament passages refer to the role and importance of pastors, deacons, and elders. None, however, give what we would call a complete and detailed job description. However, 1 Timothy 3:1-13 does describe the desired qualities of pastors (actually, overseers) and deacons.

As a group, these officers were diverse. Not all led their churches the same way. Nor did they always agree on matters of belief and doctrine. (In fact, their disagreements led to many further writings.) Some leaders had large followings due to the force of their personalities, apparent giftedness, or education; some because they had been disciples of the Apostles; others because their church was thought to have been founded by one of the Apostles; and still others because their church was in a major city.

Whatever the reason, some church leaders—usually pastors—were seen as having additional, higher authority. These became what we would call "bishops." Some today refer to them as "monarchical bishops" because they ruled. They were allowed and expected by many in the early church to determine correct teaching and practice. This way, many thought, the church would avoid confusion. The bishops would determine and explain Christian truth. The bishops would defend the faith against both heresy and persecution.

The Christian Church Becomes the Roman Empire's Church

Through the power of God, the church survived those early attacks. Despite the persecution and heresy, the church flourished. Gradually, Christianity became tolerated and, then, accepted. In fact, by the fourth century, Christianity may have had more believers than any other single religion in the Roman Empire. In AD 312, Constantine, the Roman emperor, converted to Christianity. The next year he issued the Edict of Milan, which officially removed any Roman laws that banned Christianity. Later, in 392, Theodosius declared Christianity to be the established religion of the empire.

To Christians, this may sound innocent—perhaps even desirable. However, early on, the process encountered problems and interference. Soon after the Edict of Milan, there arose a controversy over the relationship of Jesus to the Father. This and other issues threatened to split the church and, so, the empire. To avoid this, Emperor Constantine called a gathering of bishops to decide the issue and declare what was correct Christian doctrine and practice. This was the Council of Nicea, which met in AD 325. The group made many decisions, but their most important accomplishment was to establish the doctrine of the Trinity as we know it. This doctrine of the Trinity is imbedded in many of our hymns. In "Holy, Holy, Holy," we sing of "God in three persons, blessed Trinity." (It is interesting to note that the tune to which this hymn is most often sung is called "Nicea.")

So what is the problem? Actually, there are several. First, Constantine called the council. This sets the dangerous precedent of the emperor directing the church. Second, it began the trend of giving councils of bishops the authority to decide Christian doctrine and how that doctrine was required to be expressed. As more disagreements arose, more councils would meet and make similar decisions. Less and less would Christians be expected to look to Scripture for guidance in Christian belief and practice. Rather, the councils would decide. The councils, it was thought, spoke for God and were to be followed and obeyed.

The Church Is Questioned

Certainly, there were many other developments in the history of the church before Baptists. The larger structures of the Roman Catholic Church evolved, and its authority increased and widened. The church adopted the seven sacraments as the means by which God, through the church, shares grace.

However, some questioned at least parts of what had developed in the church. The Henricians of the twelfth century opposed the authority of the church, but recognized a more direct relationship between the individual and God. Likewise, the Waldenses of the same era rejected all sacraments except the Eucharist and Baptism. Two hundred years later, John Wyclif of England questioned the authority of the clergy and worked to make the Bible available in English and to all people. Later, in central Europe, John Hus followed Wyclif and questioned some church practices on the basis of Scriptural authority. John Wesel of Germany wrote that the Bible alone is the final authority in matters of faith.

The Reformation and Rise of Anabaptists

In the early sixteenth century, a Roman Catholic teacher/monk in Germany, Martin Luther, was frustrated in his search for a closer walk with God. He could not find it in the practices of the church. Finally, reading Paul's quote from Habakkuk 2:4 in Romans 1:17, he realized that passage's great truth: "the righteous man shall live by faith" (NASB). This discovery led Luther to question many of the church's teachings. Luther realized that authority in matters of faith was to be found in the Bible and not in the church, in the church's councils, or in its creeds. On October 31, 1517, Luther posted a challenge to discuss church practices. His clear intent was not to question them based on the findings of church councils. Rather, he concluded, the practices were not consistent with Scripture. This date and event are usually identified as the beginning of the Reformation.

Luther was not alone. He was followed by Ulrich Zwingli and, later, John Calvin of Switzerland. Zwingli agreed with Luther on matters of biblical authority and opposed some of the same church practices, but he saw the Eucharist (the Lord's Supper) as a symbol rather than a sacrament. Like Luther and Zwingli, Calvin claimed to rely on Scripture alone as the authority for Christian doctrine and practice. All three of these branches of the Reformation sought to establish governments based on their respective Christian beliefs. Each did this through force of arms as well as preaching, teaching, and the establishment of schools.

Two of Zwingli's followers, Conrad Grebel and George Blaurock, soon challenged their leader on two fronts. First, although he opposed the Catholic Mass, to appease those whom he felt were not so inclined, Zwingli continued the practice. Grebel challenged this, accusing Zwingli of obeying men rather than God through Scripture. Secondly, on the basis of their understanding of Scripture, Grebel and Blaurock opposed infant baptism. They and their followers refused to baptize infants. In January 1525, Grebel, Blaurock, and Felix Manz debated Zwingli on the matter before the Zurich city council. The council sided with Zwingli and ordered the three and their followers to baptize their infant children.

Though it meant exile, the group refused to obey the order. Instead, in what was an illegal meeting, the group proclaimed the New Testament the basis of their practice as Christians. As a result, Grebel baptized Blaurock and Blaurock baptized the others who had confessed faith in Jesus.

Grebel and the others were not alone. There had been like-minded Christians in Germany. Both the Swiss and the German groups—and those who followed in their footsteps—are called Radical Reformers. Certainly, they were a part of the Protestant Reformation. Among the important doctrines of the Reformation were authority of Scripture, salvation by faith, and priesthood of all believers. What set them apart was their radical application of those doctrines in their practice of the Christian faith.

They also became known as "Anabaptists." Of course, they did not oppose baptism itself. Rather, this term of scorn was given because they denied infant baptism. They believed in baptism only of believers. In fact, this is a good example of their thorough application of authority of Scripture. They found no basis for infant baptism in the Bible, so they refused the practice.

The Anabaptists' rejection of infant baptism was a serious concern for Roman Catholics and "mainline" Reformers alike. But this was not the only reason Anabaptists found trouble at the hands of the established churches.

Both the German and the Swiss Anabaptists had seen the horrible abuses of persecution when church and government were intermixed. They had seen how Roman Catholics, Lutherans, Calvinists, and others had established state churches. Whenever and wherever this had happened, the dominant religion was forced on others. Taxes, required of all, were taken for the support of the state church. People were not allowed to worship or otherwise practice their religion freely—even if it was based on scriptural principles.

The established churches were incensed. They reasoned that if a child, born with the taint of original sin, were not baptized, he/she was doomed to hell. Further, if taxes were not taken to support the state church, how would it survive? The result was persecution of Anabaptists. Some were burned at the stake, some imprisoned, and others drowned.

Still, the Anabaptist movement spread to other areas of Europe. A Dutch Roman Catholic priest, Menno Simons, began to reconsider the sacraments. At first, he thought his doubts were the work of Satan. However, he soon came under the influence of Anabaptists and was troubled even further by their teachings. Simons's fears drove him to study the Bible about the matters. His study led him to believe, for example, that the Lord's Supper is symbolic. As a result, Simons began to move closer to the Anabaptists. In 1535, Simons's brother, Peter, was among a group of Anabaptists killed in the Netherlands. A year later, Menno Simons himself formally aligned with the Anabaptists and rejected infant baptism.

Through his preaching, teaching, and writing, Menno Simons became an influential leader among the Dutch Anabaptists. So strong was Simons's influence that a major portion of the Anabaptists became known by his name: Mennonites.

Run out of the Netherlands, Germany, and Switzerland, Mennonites and other Anabaptists spread across Europe. Many went to Russia, the Ukraine, and England. Some eventually immigrated to North America.

In England, Anabaptists found a kinship with the followers of John Wyclif, known as Lollards. Like Wyclif, the Lollards stressed the authority of Scripture over that of the church through its priests. Even the Bible translator, William Tyndale, came to be identified with the Anabaptists.

However, in England, Anabaptists still met trouble. English King Henry VIII was committed in his persecution of "dissenters"—those who disagreed with any teaching and practice of the established church. He was especially harsh with Anabaptists, many of whom he had arrested and burned at the stake for heresy.

Baptists Begin, Grow, and Spread

The Rise of English Baptists

Our study of English Baptists can take us in many directions. Baptists in England expressed themselves in two basic ways: as "General Baptists" and as "Particular Baptists." There were also "Seventh Day Baptists." The histories of these groups have similarities and differences. The same is true of their respective theologies. We will begin with the background out of which both General and Particular Baptists arose. Then we will look at each group individually and consider briefly the origins of Seventh Day Baptists. Finally, we will examine both the doctrines of General and Particular Baptists and how they wrote about those beliefs and practices.

Henry VIII had separated the church in England from the Roman Catholic Church. He had also established himself and his successors as the heads of the Church of England, known as the Anglican Church. However, religious agreement eluded England. Various heirs fought over the English throne. Some were Anglican. Some were loyal Roman Catholics. When either side took the throne, they were harsh in punishing any who differed.

During this time there arose those who chose neither the Anglican nor the Roman Catholic Church as they were. These "dissenters" differed among themselves. Some did not want to leave the Church of England but purify it.

Strongly influenced by the teaching of John Calvin, these became known as "Puritans." From their ranks rose Oliver Cromwell, who led in the English Civil War. After overthrowing the English monarchy, England was established as a Commonwealth. Cromwell was its head and known as "Lord Protector." Cromwell, too, ruthlessly imposed his religious views on Roman Catholics. He was more tolerant toward Protestants. That led to the rise and growth of many differing groups.

All along, however, some dissenters had tired of attempts to reform the church from within. They wanted to leave and be independent of the state church, be it Anglican or Roman Catholic. These were the "Separatists." Robert Browne was one of the first. In 1581 Browne established a Separatist church in Norwich. Henry Barrow and John Greenwood followed in Browne's footsteps. They were arrested in 1586 for their Separatist teaching and preaching and executed seven years later.

The English Parliament eventually passed several laws to restrict the practice of Separatists. The Act of Uniformity of 1662 required worship and ordination as directed by the Anglican Church. The Quaker Act of the same year criminalized any worship other than Anglican. The Conventicle Act of 1664 forbade the assembly of more than five people for religious purposes—unless with the consent of the Anglican Church. The Five Mile Act of 1665 stated that, if the government had expelled a minister from his church, he could not live closer than five miles from that church.

Persecution of dissenters—whether Baptist, Quaker, or of another type—continued. But still they flourished. However, in 1689, the Roman Catholic King James II was overthrown. This ended many years of struggle and civil war between religious factions. The absolute power of the English monarchy also was over. The Anglican Church was finally established as the state church. In the same year, the English Parliament passed an "Act of Toleration." It allowed dissenters such as Baptists (but not Roman Catholics) to worship and teach as they pleased as long as they took oaths of allegiance to the crown. Still, they were prohibited from holding public office at any level.

The General Baptists

One of the Separatists was John Smyth. Smyth was well educated and, in 1594, had been ordained an Anglican priest. Smyth soon became disillusioned with some Anglican practices. He felt that the Anglican prayer book had become more important than Bible reading in Anglican worship.

Outspoken about this and other beliefs, Smyth was imprisoned. Finally, he broke completely with the Anglican Church. In 1606 he became pastor of an independent, dissenting church in Gainsborough. The church had recently divided as a safety move in the face of persecution, and the previous pastor had left with the new group, which moved to Scrooby. Only the layman, Thomas Helwys, remained as a leader. Helwys, a well-educated and wealthy lawyer, had been known as one who sheltered dissenters. Smyth found a refuge in Helwys's home. The congregation soon elected Smyth to replace their recently departed pastor.

It was not long before persecution pressured the Gainsborough and Scrooby congregations to move to Amsterdam in the Netherlands. At the time, Amsterdam was known as a haven for English dissenters. There the two congregations merged with a third, also comprised of English dissenters. However, some doctrinal differences arose, and Smyth, Helwys, and their followers began their own church.

Smyth became a popular preacher. He continued to study and consider his own theology. In his *Short Confession of Faith*, written in 1609, Smyth stated that infants were without sin. (To Anglicans and Catholics, this would render infants' baptism unnecessary.) He also wrote that church should have two types of leaders: pastors and deacons. He wrote of the authority of the local church.

There was a strong collection of Mennonites in Amsterdam. Smyth came to agree with these Anabaptists in practicing believer's baptism and that Jesus' death had been for all. They believed, then, in a general atonement. This is why they were called "General Baptists." Shortly before his death, Smyth describes more of his views on faith and practice in his *Propositions and Conclusions Concerning True Christian Religion.*

Smyth convinced Helwys and many others from the original Gainsborough and Scrooby groups to agree with him on many of these matters. After separating from the Anglican Church, Smyth had rebaptized himself by pouring. Later, Smyth and the others committed not only to believer's baptism, but also to baptism the way the Mennonites had practiced it: by immersion.

However, Smyth attempted to merge his congregation with the Mennonites. The Mennonites rebuffed him. This was a bit too much for Helwys and some of the others. They parted ways with Smyth. Smyth remained in Amsterdam and ministered there until his death in 1612.

About that time, however, Helwys and John Murton led a group of about eleven to return to England. They settled in Spitalfields, then located just outside the city walls of London. Now it is near the center of London. This was the first Baptist Church on English soil. (Coincidentally, it had been the site of a Roman Catholic monastery and hospital that, earlier, had been closed by Henry VIII.)

The move was bold, for they had returned to the place that would not tolerate dissenters. But Helwys went a huge step further. Around the time of this return, he wrote *A Short Declaration of the Mystery of Iniquity*. In fact, it was actually a long letter addressed to King James I, the king who had authorized the translation of the Bible that carries his name. Helwys dared to send the king an autographed copy. It was a call for religious liberty and the separation of church and state. Though he pledged his loyalty to the king, Helwys also wrote, "The King is a mortal man and not God, therefore hath no power over immortal souls of his subjects."

This simple statement resulted in Helwys's arrest. He was locked in a cell in Newgate Prison. He died there in either 1615 or 1616. John Murton succeeded Helwys as pastor of the church. Like Helwys, Murton addressed the issue of religious liberty for all. Writing to the king in his *A Most Humble Supplication*, Murton declared, "Far be it from you to sit in the consciences of men . . . ."[2] In 1615 Murton wrote *Persecution for Religions Judg'd and Condemn'd*, saying that any who would force religion on others would be judged by God. Murton's belief was that the Bible alone, inspired by God, should be the authority over one's conscience. He wrote, "The rule of faith is the doctrine of the Holy Ghost contained in sacred Scriptures, and not any church, council, prince, or potentate, nor any man whatsoever."[3] In 1615, Murton wrote *Persecution for Religions Judg'd and Condemn'd*, saying that any who would force religion on others would be judged by God.[4] Not surprisingly, the authorities arrested and jailed Murton for his beliefs. Being a "good Baptist," Murton proved to be stubborn. Even from his prison cell, he wrote to share his beliefs. He was able to smuggle his writings out of jail by using milk as "ink." This made his writing invisible when dry. However, when the paper was held up to light, the writing could be read.

Particular Baptists

As stated above, Particular Baptists were those who arose out of the Puritan, rather than the Separatist, tradition. They were more Calvinistic. That is, they agreed with the theology of John Calvin, one of the important leaders of the Protestant Reformation. One distinct feature of Calvin's theology was the belief in limited or particular atonement. That means that Jesus' sacrifice was not for everyone. The Calvinists believed that, though all people were/are sinners, God had selected certain ones to go to hell. Therefore, Jesus' atoning death was not for them. Jesus' sacrifice was only for those whom God had predestined (chosen ahead of time) to be saved.

In 1616 there was an "independent" Anglican congregation in London that had Puritan leanings. Up to that point, this congregation had chosen not to separate fully from the Church. That year, however, they did. The pastor was Henry Jacob. At first, they were not opposed to infant baptism. However, through the leadership of a succession of pastors (Henry Jacob, John Lathrop, and Henry Jessey), they thought about the issue. By 1638 the church began to teach only believer's baptism. However, like the General Baptists at first, they baptized by pouring.

A few years later, this Particular Baptist church sent Richard Blunt to Amsterdam to discuss baptism with the Mennonites. Blunt and his church became convinced that immersion was the proper, New Testament mode of baptism. At this point historians differ. Some state that the Mennonites immersed Blunt. Others suggest that he baptized himself. They agree, however, that Blunt returned to baptize the others of his congregation.

John Bunyan, preacher and author of the classic *Pilgrim's Progress*, was a Particular Baptist. He was baptized in a Baptist church in Bedford in 1653. There he became a deacon and began his preaching ministry. Eventually, Bunyan was arrested for preaching without governmental permission. In 1660 he began what was to be a three-month prison term. However, Bunyan refused to quit preaching. The result was that his imprisonment lasted twelve years. Bunyan's release was due to King Charles II's decree of "religious indulgence." With this act, Charles II intended to begin the reestablishment of the Roman Catholic Church in England.

Upon his release, Bunyan became pastor of the Bedford church. Just three years later, however, Charles II withdrew his act of indulgence. Bunyan once again was jailed for his preaching. This term lasted only six months.

Seventh Day Baptists

There was also among the English Baptists a group known as Seventh Day Baptists. They began in the 1650s. Many of this group came from among General Baptists, but some had been Particular Baptists. As their name suggests, they differed from other English Baptists mostly on the matter of

Sabbath worship. To them it was a matter of adherence to biblical teaching. They thought Genesis 2 and the Ten Commandments established the Sabbath as holy. God's law at that point, they believed, had not changed.

Peter Chamberlain was a physician and a leader in a General Baptist church in Lothbury. Many of that church followed him in adhering to seventh-day beliefs and practices. The whole group relocated to Mill Yard and there founded Mill Yard Seventh Day General Baptist Church. As a physician, Chamberlain had been concerned with many issues related to public health. As a Christian and Baptist, however, he was distressed by squabbling among Christians. He called for Christians to focus more on what they had in common and less on issues about which they differed.

Francis Bampfield was a Seventh Day Baptist pastor. Though a Royalist and an Anglican minister, he had refused to vow allegiance to the government. He served nine years in prison for that offense. Even during his imprisonment, Bampfield kept preaching. During this time, he accepted Seventh Day Baptist beliefs. After his release from prison, Bampfield baptized himself. He married in the Mill Yard Seventh Day Baptist Church. Though an itinerant preacher, Bampfield founded a church in Bethel Green. Still refusing to take the oath of allegiance, he was again imprisoned. He died in Newgate Prison in 1684—nearly seventy years after Thomas Helwys suffered the same fate in the same place.

The English Baptists Differ

We have seen that both strains of English Baptists were misunderstood and persecuted. It was common for Baptist bodies, then, to draft statements of faith. These were not creeds; that would have violated the basic Baptist premise that only the Bible is authoritative in matters of Christian faith and practice. A creed also supposes that it may be imposed on another. However, Baptists held firmly that no person could command another in matters of conscience. Therefore, that imposition, too, was alien to Baptist beliefs. Rather, Baptists meant for their confessions to explain Baptist beliefs and practices. These purposes were like those of the apologists of the early Christian church. They also serve to show how those English Baptists differed.

General Baptist confessions find some of their origins in faith statements of their early leaders. John Smyth's *Short Confession of Faith* and *Propositions and Conclusions Concerning True Christian Religion* are examples, as is Thomas Helwys's *Declaration of Faith*, written in 1611.

Soon, however, General Baptists began to make corporate statements. The first of these was *Faith and Practice of Thirty Congregations.* Messengers from thirty different Baptist churches joined together in 1651 to write it. Forty-five of its paragraphs were statements of belief. Thirty of them focused on church practice. One of the most significant sections developed the basis for soul competency.[5]

The *Standard Confession* of 1660 is a clear statement of the General Baptists' beliefs about atonement, believer's baptism by immersion, roles of pastors and deacons, freedom of religion, and congregational polity. The *Orthodox Creed* of 1678, though professing belief in general atonement and free will, sounded a bit Calvinist regarding election. It used the term "sacraments" in affirming two ordinances: believer's baptism by immersion and Lord's Supper. It also emphasized the local church, but stated awareness of the church universal. It stressed local church governance. This confession equated elders with pastors and recognized the role of deacons as those who were to serve the poor. It also recognized another church office—that of bishops! However, in this case, bishops (or "overseers") actually were more of an ordination council.

The Particular Baptists were inclined to develop confessions of faith. However, they eventually developed and published three of special importance. These statements of faith help us understand their beliefs and practices. Some Particular Baptist churches were concerned that many had accused them of agreeing with certain Anabaptists. Among the charges were that they believed in free will and opposed baptism. Others related to their views on governmental authority. So, in 1644, seven Particular Baptist churches in London joined together to write the *First London Confession of Faith.* William Kiffin and Hanserd Knollys, two leaders among Particular Baptists, led in writing it. As expected, the *First London Confession*—and its 1646 version—claimed limited atonement and other Calvinist beliefs regarding election, original sin, total depravity, irresistible grace, among others. It also described a church as a body made up of baptized believers. It described churches as self-governing. Churches were encouraged to support the ministers they had chosen. Important to note is that it was written sixteen years before the General Baptists' *Standard Confession.* That makes the *First London Confession* the first Baptist statement to be written by a group of churches. It was also the first to affirm baptism by immersion.

In 1655, a group of Particular Baptist churches from Wales and the midlands of England produced what is known as the *Midland Confession.* It was similar in theology to the *First London Confession*, but it was much briefer. The most Calvinistic Particular Baptist statement was the *Second London Confession of Faith*. It was written in 1689 and seems to have been based on the Church of Scotland's 1647 *Westminster Confession*.

Andrew Fuller was a Particular Baptist who paved the way for even more Calvinistic Baptists to be evangelistic. Born in 1754, Fuller was saved and baptized at the age of sixteen after being influenced by watching the baptisms of two friends. He became active in the Soham Baptist Church, which ordained and called him as their pastor in 1775. Fuller pastored that church seven years before being called to pastor the Kettering church, where he served until his death. Though a Particular Baptist and Calvinist in theological orientation, Fuller did not feel that limited atonement precluded inviting others to accept the gospel. He died in Kettering in 1815.

Fuller influenced William Carey, another important figure among English Baptists. Carey is best known as the "Father of Baptist Missions." His story is wonderful and powerful. However, it also illustrates some of the tensions that arose among English Baptists. Carey was born into the Anglican Church in 1761 but became a Baptist in 1783. He was ordained as a minister in 1787 and became pastor of the Baptist church in Moulton.

A cobbler by trade, Carey was a voracious reader and became self-educated. He read many writings of the famous explorer, Captain James Cook. Cook's writings inspired Carey to teach himself several languages. He also became concerned about missions.

Carey began to preach to his church and fellow ministers about missions responsibility. At a pastor's conference in 1787, he proposed that the group discuss whether the Great Commission Jesus gave to His disciples was binding on all succeeding ministers and pastors. An older fellow pastor, Dr. Ryland, a staunch Calvinist, rebuked him, saying, "Sit down, young man. You are an enthusiast! When God pleases to convert the heathen, He will do it without consulting you or me." This statement did not deter Carey, but serves to illustrate how Calvinist theology could and did influence religious thinking among some English Baptists.

Five years later, in 1792, Carey preached in an associational meeting from Isaiah 54:2-3. He concluded his sermon with the famous (among Baptists) phrase: "Expect great things—attempt great things." However, some of the Particular Baptists felt that missions was not central to the task of the church. Thus, no action was taken.

Carey was still not daunted. Later that year, at the home of a widowed Mrs. Wallis in Kettering, Carey led a group of pastors to establish, along with Andrew Fuller, the British Missionary Society, originally known as "The Particular Baptist Society for Propagating the Gospel among the Heathen." The next year Carey was appointed its first missionary. He raised the necessary funds and sailed—with his wife and four children—for India.

Particular Baptists and General Baptists differed on issues other than atonement. For example, they disagreed about worship—especially how Psalms should be sung. General Baptists were reluctant to sing hymns, because human hands wrote them. John Gill, a Particular Baptist, supported the singing of both Psalms and hymns—and the hymns only as long as they were consistent with Scripture. Some General Baptist churches laid hands on new believers. They believed this was in keeping with the practice of the early church as indicated in Acts and Hebrews. Others disagreed, stating that there was no command in the Bible for the practice. Despite these many areas of disagreement, in 1891, General and Particular Baptists united as Baptist Union of Great Britain and Ireland.

Baptists Come to North America

Religion in the North American British Colonies

As Britain colonized North America, the churches and religious differences came along. The first North American British colony, Jamestown, Virginia, was established in 1607. Law decreed the Anglican Church to be the state church. The same happened as most other colonies began. A bishop in England appointed ministers to those colonial Anglican churches. The government imposed taxes to support Anglican ministers and churches.

Maryland's history differs from Virginia's. George Calvert, Lord Baltimore, was a Roman Catholic. He established Maryland in 1632 for trade and profit and as a refuge for British Roman Catholics. However, he died before the new colony actually began. The colonial charter was granted to Lord Baltimore's son, Cecilius. Another son, Leonard, became Maryland's first governor. Leonard knew that the colony's financial success depended on the cooperation and good will of Protestants settling there. For Roman Catholics to receive tolerance, they would need to extend it to others. In 1649 Maryland's assembly passed "An Act Concerning Religion." Most know it as the Maryland Toleration Act of 1649. It required toleration of all Christian expressions of faith. The result was that Maryland became the most diverse colony in terms of religion. Subsequently, Maryland's colonial status changed to that of a "royal province." In 1691 one result was that Maryland established the Anglican Church as the state church. This soon led to religious persecution—especially of Roman Catholics—and, so, the religious diversity envisioned by Maryland's founders.

Like the Baptists and other dissenters in England, the Quakers had suffered much persecution. William Penn became one of their leaders and wrote many pamphlets and books calling for religious toleration. He saw the British colonies as a place where Quakers and others could escape oppression. In 1677, Penn worked to relocate a group of Quakers to New Jersey. Four years later, he received a charter to establish the colony of Pennsylvania. He called it "a Holy Experiment"—a place where all could worship as they saw fit.

The "pilgrims" of *Mayflower* fame established the colony of Massachusetts at Plymouth in 1620. Most were Puritans, but some were Separatists who had connections with John Smyth's Gainsborough church. Early on, the Massachusetts colony accepted diverse religious views, but as the Puritan (Calvinist) population became the majority, that acceptance eroded. At first, tensions rose between the Puritan leaders and any who differed. In 1644 and 1646, Massachusetts passed laws against Baptists and any others who opposed infant baptism and other teachings of the established church.

The First Baptists in America

Roger Williams was born in England in 1599 near Newgate, where various English Baptist leaders were imprisoned. He studied to be a lawyer but became an Anglican priest. However, Williams became disillusioned with the Anglican Church and began to identify with the Puritans. In 1631, he and his wife, Mary, followed the earlier Puritan group to Massachusetts. He eventually became an associate pastor and teacher at the church in Plymouth.

Soon, two matters became important to Williams. One related to Massachusetts' treatment of Native American tribes in the area. The colony had taken Native American land—without compensation. He felt that Native Americans should be treated fairly and with dignity and respect. The second issue related to freedom of conscience. In 1631 Williams had read John Murton's *A Most Humble Supplication* (mentioned above). As a result, Williams became convicted that a person could know only his/her personal conscience and no one else's.

Williams began to preach and teach his convictions about religious liberty and the maltreatment of Native Americans. In 1635 Massachusetts issued an order banishing Williams from the colony. The civil authorities wanted to send him back to England, but Williams went away on his own. Native Americans in the area gave him refuge for several months. Williams soon purchased land from the Narragansett and named the settlement Providence. This was the beginning of the colony of Rhode Island. Made up of both General and Particular Baptists, the church Williams started there is considered the first Baptist church in America. However, even more significant is that Williams established the colony explicitly as a refuge for people of all faiths and free from religious persecution and pressure. Rhode Island soon became exactly that. It was a place where Quakers and other Christian dissenters could worship as they saw fit. It was also the home of the first Jewish synagogue in America.

John Clarke is not as well known as Roger Williams, but he was a part of the founding of Rhode Island. Some would even argue that it was he, not Roger Williams, who was the true founder of Baptists in America. Williams became a "Seeker." Looking for a further revelation from God, he parted with the Baptist church in Providence a few months (perhaps weeks) after its founding. Clarke remained. Ultimately, the charter for the colony of Rhode Island was issued to Clarke.

Clarke was born in England in 1609. He studied both medicine and theology. A Puritan by conviction, he immigrated to Massachusetts in 1637. He agreed with Williams in numerous ways. Clarke, too, championed religious freedom. He also joined Williams in buying land that was to become part of Rhode Island. Clarke established Portsmouth in 1638. It was there that Clarke joined with others in signing the "Portsmouth Compact." This document stated their intent to establish religious freedom for all. Clarke also founded Newport in 1639 and started a church there. He became the pastor of that church, supporting himself through his practice of medicine.

In 1651 Clarke, along with Obadiah Holmes and John Crandall, was arrested in Lynn, Massachusetts, for conducting an unauthorized worship service in a private home there. They were accused of being Anabaptists. This they denied, for they were not "against" baptism. Nevertheless, the three were fined. Only Holmes declined to pay his fine. The result for Holmes was a public whipping—thirty-nine lashes—in Boston.

Another result of this incident was Clarke's writing, in 1652, a pamphlet exposing the religious persecution taking place in Massachusetts. The short title of the work is *Ill Newes [News] from New England.* In it Clarke not only told the story of the abuses, but also outlined his beliefs regarding theology and church practice. Clarke described baptism as an outward sign for the believer—and it should be by immersion. Clarke also argued for complete freedom of conscience and religion.

Despite Clarke's best efforts, persecution in Massachusetts continued. In 1640, Henry Dunster, a clergyman in Boston, was appointed the first president of the new Harvard College (known at first as Cambridge College). Due to the witness of Clarke, Crandall, and Holmes, Dunster studied the biblical teaching on baptism. He became convinced of Baptist beliefs regarding infant baptism. When his son was born in 1653, Dunster refused to have the infant baptized. After a yearlong controversy, Dunster resigned his presidency. Forced out of his home, he moved to Scituate where he served as pastor in a small church until his death five years later at the age of forty-seven.

Dunster's witness, in turn, influenced many people, including his friend Thomas Goold. Goold lived in Charleston and, in 1655, refused to present his child for baptism. For ten years the established state church, in the hope that Goold would give in, imposed restrictions on his worship and fellowship. During that time, Goold gathered like-minded believers in his home for fellowship. After his continuing refusal to accept infant baptism, Goold was expelled from the church. In response, Goold and others founded a Baptist church—First Baptist Church of Boston.

First Baptist Church of Boston became a model followed by many Baptist churches. William Screven had been born in England in 1629. As an adult, he immigrated to New England. He soon sympathized with Baptist views and worked as a merchant living in Kittery in what is now Maine. He and another Kittery man, Humphrey Churchwood, asked to be baptized by First Baptist Church of Boston in 1681. The church agreed. The next year, Churchwood wrote FBC Boston a letter asking them to establish a church in Kittery. The church did so and ordained Screven as the pastor. The small, new Baptist church in Kittery would not find peace, however. Screven and others were fined, imprisoned, and otherwise harassed for not attending worship at a recognized church and for speaking out against infant baptism. Finally, in 1696, twenty-eight members of the church moved to Cooper Creek, South Carolina, near what is now Charleston. They became First Baptist Church of Charleston and the first Baptist church in the South. Both later had a tremendous influence on Baptists of the American South.

Another such influence finds its roots in the leadership and preaching of Shubal Stearns. Stearns was born in 1706 in Boston. He was converted in 1745 under the preaching of George Whitefield, a great revival preacher of the day. Whitefield preached and taught that true believers must be "true lights" guiding the true church back to the right path as directed by God. This meant they should separate from the established church. Stearns agreed and soon came to oppose infant baptism and hold to believer's baptism. Stearns became what was known as a "Separate Baptist" and was baptized by a Baptist minister in Connecticut.

Stearns gathered a significant number of followers. He moved with some of them to what was then the western frontier—Virginia. The group had trouble getting along with even some of the other Baptists there who saw them as too radical. Stearns and his followers moved on to the Sandy Creek area of North Carolina. There they established a church and an association of Baptist churches. Both the Sandy Creek Church and the Sandy Creek Association emphasized revival, conviction, and conversion. These would be the foundations for the Sandy Creek Tradition.

Richard Furman was born in New York and graduated from the Baptist Rhode Island College, now known as Brown University. Furman had a heritage influenced by Shubal Stearns. It was one of an evangelistic Calvinism. Furman became pastor of First Baptist Church of Charleston. These were the years of the American Revolution, and Furman urged many to join the colonial revolutionary cause. Furman was such an American patriot that the British General Cornwallis even offered a bounty for his capture.

Though he was supportive of education, Furman's influence on Baptist life goes beyond the South Carolina university that bears his name. He was a strong and vocal advocate of religious freedom. Only through absolute religious liberty, he thought, could one experience true faith. Furman agitated to strike down the Anglican Church as the state church of South Carolina. It was a matter of both freedom of conscience and freeing the state from British influence.

He also saw the need for Baptist churches, though independent and autonomous, to cooperate with each other on certain matters and purposes. Furman was a driving force in the founding of cooperative missions in the Charleston Association and the organization of the South Carolina Baptist Convention.

Baptist leader John Leland had a similar influence. However, his is felt even today not only by Baptists, but by all citizens of the United States.

Leland was born in 1754 in Grafton, Massachusetts. His home was Christian, his father being a Presbyterian and his mother a separate new-light Christian (much like George Whitefield mentioned above). However, John Leland was baptized at the age of twenty in a Baptist church and the next year joined a Baptist church in Bellingham, Massachusetts.

Leland became a Baptist minister and served churches in Massachusetts and Virginia. Most of his life and energies were spent preaching and otherwise serving as a minister. Among Leland's greatest passions were religious liberty and the right relationship between church and state. Toward that end, Leland became involved in politics. He knew personally many of the "founding fathers" of the United States. Among those whom he knew especially well and influenced were Thomas Jefferson and James Madison. Leland's belief in freedom of conscience also ultimately led to his opposing slavery.

As a pastor and a leader among Baptists in Virginia, Leland influenced Jefferson's Bill for Religious Freedom of 1785. He also supported Madison's call for a new constitution. However, Leland did not grant that support until he had received from Madison the guarantee that the new constitution would include a bill of rights, which would, in turn, guarantee religious freedom and separation of church and state. This led to the inclusion of the First Amendment in the U. S. Constitution's Bill of Rights.

Leland preached his last sermon on January 14, 1841, in Cheshire, Massachusetts, and died six days later. However, his legacy extends to Americans today through the Constitution. His witness also continues through those to whom he ministered. It is summarized on his tombstone: "Here lies the body of John Leland, who labored 67 years to promote piety and vindicate the civil and religious rights of all men."

Baptists in America Work Together

Like their English forebears, Baptist churches in North America believed each church to be independent and autonomous, or self-ruling. As a fellowship of baptized believers (and a local "kingdom of priests"), each church was free to decide who could be a member, how members were to be disciplined, and who would serve as the church's officers and ministers. Wisely, they were reluctant to give up those freedoms. However, they also realized that there were times when it was wise for autonomous Baptist churches to band together for a common purpose. In fact, one article in the above-mentioned *First London Confession* of 1644 made that statement. (As already noted, the *First London Confession* was itself a joint statement of an association of

Particular Baptist Churches.) This understanding prevailed among English Baptists. For reasons of mutual support and the benefits of presenting a united front, groups of their churches organized into associations.

Also like their English predecessors, Baptist churches in North America often joined with other, like-minded churches in annual meetings. These were times of mutual support and encouragement, preaching, teaching, and dialogue on matters of doctrine and practice. In 1707, five such churches in Philadelphia, Pennsylvania, went a step further. They organized into the first Baptist association in North America. It had a tremendous influence on subsequent associations and Baptist churches in the middle and southern colonies and, later, states.

Other associations began, and most published their own statements of faith. The Philadelphia Association and others also issued what they called "circular letters." This common practice was a way for associations of churches to counsel other churches and discuss issues of common concern. The practice led to theological similarity while respecting congregational independence. Associations continued as the basic Baptist organization beyond that of the local church.

Baptist churches and associations also began to join together as state conventions. Like local or area associations, these state conventions were formed for mutual support, education, and encouragement as well as for the purposes of missions and other ways of spreading the gospel. The earliest effort toward this end was established in North Carolina in 1812, but it did not last long (a more permanent state convention in North Carolina began in 1830). The first permanent convention was the South Carolina state convention, which started in 1821. Baptists in other states followed suit: Virginia and Alabama in 1823 and Georgia in 1827. State conventions served as the means by which Baptist churches could work together for common purposes. Tensions remained, however. Some disagreed over doctrinal issues. Other disagreements concerned how the state convention could operate effectively while still respecting local church autonomy.

The first national organization of Baptists had its roots in a fellowship of college students. Williams College was a Congregationalist school in Massachusetts. At Williams in the early 1800s, a group of students became interested in missions. Their practice was to pray together regularly regarding spiritual growth, ministry, and missions. In 1806, a thunderstorm disrupted one of their prayer meetings. The group took refuge in a haystack—a foolish move by today's understanding. Nevertheless, that prayer meeting had a powerful influence on the students. They resolved to put feet to their prayers and committed themselves to be forces for missions. They exerted a tremendous influence on one of their friends who had not been at the "Haystack Prayer Meeting." His name was Luther Rice.

After graduating from Williams, Rice entered Andover Seminary to study to become a missionary. There he met Adoniram Judson, who, in 1810, had accepted the call to missions and had recently graduated from Brown University. He also met Ann Hasseltine, who had graduated from Bradford Academy. Adoniram and Ann eventually married. The couple joined with Rice in committing themselves to missions. In 1812 the three were commissioned as missionaries and set sail for India.

The trio knew that they would likely encounter the Baptist missionary William Carey. Coming from churches that practiced infant baptism, they knew they would need to be prepared to discuss— and even debate—the matter. On the voyage across the Atlantic, they studied the New Testament teaching regarding baptism. Their study convinced them that only believer's baptism was biblical.

As a result, the group chose to go to Burma instead of India. They also sought support from Baptists rather than from Congregationalists. Rice soon returned to the United States. On his one-eyed horse, Columbus, Rice rode up and down the eastern seaboard, telling Baptist churches about the Judsons and their work.

Rice's meetings with the Charleston Association (in 1813) and others led to an 1814 meeting of Baptists at First Baptist Church in Philadelphia. Some were from various missions societies that already existed. Some were from churches, others from certain associations. There and then, this Baptist group founded the "General Missionary Convention of the Baptist Denomination in the United States for Foreign Missions." It became known as the Triennial Convention because it was to meet every three years. Richard Furman of South Carolina was its first president. The convention was established for the support of the Judsons and others called to foreign missions. Toward that end, the Triennial Convention requested an annual donation of $100 from each participating organization. That may seem a small amount to most churches today, but the dollar value was significantly more at the time.

The Triennial Convention soon expanded its interests to include domestic, or home, missions. There arose other societies with varied areas of concern such as missions, educational materials, and Baptist journals.

The Triennial Convention was born in a time when slavery was becoming increasingly controversial. Not surprisingly, some of its leaders supported slavery. Richard Furman was one. Others were abolitionists. Still others, such as Francis Wayland, opposed slavery but did not want the issue to interfere with the Triennial Convention's missions enterprise. For several years there was a power struggle among the factions. Finally, in 1844, the Triennial Convention refused to endorse for home missions a slaveholder from Georgia. That same year the Triennial Convention also denied the Alabama Convention's request that it approve slaveholders as foreign missionaries.

Outraged, the Virginia Baptist Convention called for a meeting of Baptists from across the South. Messengers from various Baptist bodies—associations, societies, state conventions, and churches alike—met at First Baptist Church in Augusta, Georgia, in May 1845. The result was a split from the Triennial Convention that became known as the Southern Baptist Convention. Among the more significant resolutions passed at that first meeting was the establishment of a "Board of Managers for Foreign Missions and also one for Domestic Missions."[6]

Baptists in America Share—and Differ in—Their Beliefs

Just as the majority of English Baptists belonged to one of two groups, so it was with Baptists in the early United States. The names for the U.S. groups were "Regular" and "Separate" Baptists. Both groups were somewhat Calvinistic. However, the Regular Baptists were much more like the English Particular Baptists. This was true in their view of election and the atonement. It was also true regarding worship.

Separate Baptists were a looser group. Their worship style was more emotional and freewheeling. The Separates distrusted associations, considering them dangerous to congregational independence. They were also less apt to adopt confessions. Their concern was that confessions might be used like creeds and detract from scriptural authority. Separate Baptists also differed from the Regulars in that they required profession of faith before baptism. Sometimes Regular and Separate Baptists worked together. Often they could not or did not. Some churches counted persons from both groups among their members.

The churches of the Philadelphia Association were mostly of the Particular Baptist tradition. It is no surprise, then, that when they wanted to issue a statement of their beliefs, they turned to the *Second London Confession* of 1684. In 1747, one of their ministers, Benjamin Keach, made slight modifications to the earlier document. The statement of faith adopted by the association became known as the *Philadelphia Confession*. Although they, too, were Calvinistic by orientation, Separate Baptists refused to accept the *Philadelphia Confession*. Nevertheless, the *Philadelphia Confession* influenced the beliefs of many later Baptists. The Southern Baptist Theological Seminary adopted—under the leadership of its first president, James P. Boyce—Articles of Faith that echoed the *Philadelphia Confession*.

Though reluctant to construct statements of faith, less Calvinistic Baptists did find occasion to do so. Within the Baptist Convention of New Hampshire, tensions arose about both the atonement and missions. These New Hampshire Baptists were more from the English General Baptist tradition and wanted to distance themselves theologically from their Calvinist brethren. In 1833 the Baptist Convention of New Hampshire developed the *New Hampshire Confession of Faith*. This statement moved away from the *Philadelphia Confession*'s stand on election. Instead, it stated that salvation was free to all. Further, it described election in terms of God's design or plan of salvation and regeneration. However, the *New Hampshire Confession* did agree with the *Philadelphia Confession* on perseverance of the saints ("once saved always saved"). The *New Hampshire Confession* described church as a fellowship of baptized believers. It also held that the ordinances of baptism and the Lord's Supper are important reminders of the work of Jesus Christ in the life of the individual and in the life of the church. Important to note is that the *New Hampshire Confession* became the most widely accepted statement of faith among Baptists of the American South. Southwestern Baptist Theological Seminary, the second Southern Baptist seminary, even adopted it in 1908 as its Articles of Faith.

Further, even the leadership of the Southern Baptist Theological Seminary eventually shifted from the more Calvinist Boyce to the less Calvinist Edgar Young Mullins. Mullins chaired and strongly influenced the committee that wrote the 1925 *Baptist Faith and Message*. This statement was based on the *New Hampshire Confession*. The subsequent 1963 statement only slightly modified the 1925 version.

The differing views among Baptists regarding the atonement led to yet other differences in practice. An anti-missionary movement arose among Baptists. It began mostly with Daniel Parker, who was born in Virginia in 1781. He grew up in Georgia and converted at age twenty-one. He was ordained to ministry in Tennessee two years later. Parker's Calvinist theology evolved into a view that missions efforts were both futile and unnecessary.

Parker spread his teaching through his preaching in Illinois and Texas, and his ideas took root among some Baptist churches and associations there.

Another dissenting movement that touched Baptists was the Restoration Movement. Restoration was an early-1800s attempt by Thomas and Alexander Campbell—a father-and-son team—to recapture the practices and beliefs of the New Testament church. They first left Presbyterianism and joined some Baptist churches and associations in Pennsylvania and Ohio. Like Baptists, they emphasized baptism and autonomy of the local church. They were also anti-creedal and rejected the *Philadelphia Confession* as a work of human rather than divine origin. However, they became so rigid on local church autonomy that they opposed even voluntary cooperation among Baptist churches. Their opposition to this kind of denominationalism led them away from Baptists. The Campbells and their followers, often known as "Campbellites," gave rise to today's Churches of Christ and Disciples of Christ churches.

Landmarkism, an additional effort in Baptist life to reestablish the earliest church, began in 1854. One of its initial leaders was J. R. Graves of Nashville, Tennessee. An ally was J. M. Pendleton, pastor of First Baptist Church in Bowling Green, Kentucky. Graves's influence was exerted mostly through *The Tennessee Baptist*, a periodical of which he was editor. Graves encouraged Pendleton to write the tract *An Old Landmark Reset*. This writing gave the movement its name.

Graves and Pendleton not only opposed infant baptism; they also doubted that *any* church or minister who practiced or *had* practiced infant baptism could be considered truly Christian. Further, they believed only Baptist churches could lay legitimate claim to be New Testament churches. Therefore, the only place where the ordinances could be administered was in a local Baptist church. According to Landmarkism, baptism in any other church—even believer's baptism by immersion—was alien. Likewise, when a local church celebrated the Lord's Supper, only members of that church could participate. This is still known as "closed communion."

Other doctrinal and practical differences led to many divisions and to the rise of various Baptist groups in the United States. American Baptist Churches grew out of the Triennial Convention after the Southern Baptists split. There remained General Baptists, who claim descent from English forebears of the same name. Around the turn of the eighteenth century, several Separate and Regular Baptist groups joined together as United Baptists. Reformed Baptists, Seventh Day Baptists, Freewill Baptists, Primitive

Baptists, Two-Seed-in-the-Spirit Predestinarian, American Baptist Association, and many others also developed.

There are also numerous African-American Baptist conventions. A few are the National Baptist Convention USA, Inc.; the National Baptist Convention in America, Inc.; and the National Missionary Baptist Convention.

One other primarily African-American Baptist organization bears mention. The Lott Carey Foreign Mission Convention is named for a slave who became a Baptist preacher and later purchased his own freedom. Lott Carey developed an interest in missions. The Triennial Convention sent him to the new nation of Liberia, which was being populated by freed slaves. There he started the Providence Baptist Church in Monrovia. He also preached, started schools, and governed. Carey died in 1828 at the age of forty-eight. The convention that bears his named began in 1897 in Washington, D.C., for the explicit purpose of ministering in Africa.

Still other Baptist groups arose as the result of the various waves of immigrants coming to the United States. Swedish immigrants influenced by Baptists formed the Baptist General Conference. German Baptists were the seed for what became the North American Baptist Conference. Immigrants also established the Russian-Ukrainian Union of Evangelical Christians-Baptists, U.S.A. Yet others arose as Baptists evangelized specific ethnic groups (Japanese, Chinese, Hispanic, et al.).

So where do we come from? Frankly, we come from all over! Our history shows that we have many roots, stems, and branches. But we do have many things in common. Despite these differing roots and more than a few differing theological perspectives, there are some common marks of being Baptist. We will examine them in the next chapter.

Notes

[1] Frank S. Mead, *Handbook of Denominations in the United States*, 10th ed., rev. Samuel S. Hill (Nashville: Abingdon Press, 1995), 8–9.

[2] Thomas Helwys, *A Short Declaration of the Mystery of Iniquity*, Classics of Religious Liberty 1, ed. Richard Groves (Macon GA: Mercer University Press, 1998), xxiv.

[3] John Murton, *A Most Humble Supplication* (1620), in *Tracts on Liberty of Conscience and Persecution* (1614–1661), ed. Edward B. Underhill (London: Hanserd Knollys Society, 1846), 230.

[4] Ibid., 193.

[5] These works can be found at http://baptiststudiesonline.com/?page_id=7.

[6] *Proceedings of the Southern Baptist Convention Held in Augusta, Georgia, May 8th, 9th, 10th, 11th, and 12th, 1845* (Richmond VA: H. K. Ellyson, Printer, 1845), 14.

Study Questions

1. Match each statement below with the name of the person or place it best describes.

___ John Wyclif
___ First Baptist Church, Charleston, SC
___ Conrad Grebel
___ Shubal Stearns
___ John Smyth
___Richard Furman
___Thomas Helwys
___ John Leland
___ Particular Baptist
___ Philadelphia, PA
___ General Baptists
___ North Carolina
___ Andrew Fuller
___ South Carolina
___ William Carey
___ Adoniram Judson
___ Roger Williams
___ Luther Rice
___ John Clarke
___ The Triennial Convention
___ Henry Dunster
___ First Baptist Church, Augusta, GA
___ First Baptist Church, Boston, MA

A. This Baptist leader was such an American patriot that British General Cornwallis offered a bounty for his capture. He supported education, religious freedom, and cooperation among Baptist churches.
B. These early English Baptists believed Jesus died for everyone (general atonement).
C. The "Father of Baptist Missions," this cobbler/pastor later went as a missionary to India.
D. Harvard's first president, he was forced from his position for accepting Baptist beliefs.

E. At first an Anglican priest, he later became one of the first English Baptists, opposed infant baptism, and led his congregation to Amsterdam.

F. He questioned the authority of the clergy and worked to make the Bible available in English.

G. In 1845, the Southern Baptist Convention was founded here when Baptists of the South split with the Triennial Convention over the issue of slavery.

H. This Baptist organization arose out of Luther Rice's work to encourage support for missions.

I. He and his wife, Ann, became Baptists as they began their missionary careers.

J. An early Anabaptist, along with George Blaurock, he opposed the Catholic Mass and infant baptism on the basis of his understanding of Scripture.

K. An Anglican priest and teacher, he was expelled from the Massachusetts colony for preaching and teaching Baptist doctrine and championing fair treatment of Native Americans.

L. The oldest continuously functioning state Baptist convention in North America was started here.

M. A layman and one of the first English Baptists, he wrote King James I calling for religious liberty and the separation of church and state.

N. Strongly influenced by John Calvin, these early English Baptists believed Jesus died only for those God had predestined to save (limited atonement).

O. Along with Roger Williams, he was a part of the founding of Rhode Island. Some argue that he, not Roger Williams, was the true founder of Baptists in America.

P. The first Baptist church in the American South, this church began when the Baptist church in Kittery, Maine, was forced to move due to persecution.

Q. This Baptist leader's passion for religious liberty and the right relationship between church and state led him to become involved in politics. He influenced both Thomas Jefferson and James Madison and, through them, the U.S. Constitution.

R. The first state Baptist convention in North America was started here.

S. At first a missionary companion of the Judsons, he returned to the U.S. to raise support for them among Baptists.

T. Founded by Thomas Goold and others, this church supported William Screven in starting a Baptist church in Kittery, Maine.

U. He is credited with starting the Sandy Creek tradition of Baptists, which was marked by revival, conviction, and conversion.

V. This is the site of the 1707 founding of the oldest Baptist association in North America.

W. This English Particular Baptist pastor encouraged evangelism and missions work and helped start the British Missionary Society.

2. How are the confessions, creeds, and clergy of the church examples of good intentions that sometimes lead to problems?

_____

_____

_____

_____

3. What do you think were the biggest barriers early Baptists had to overcome? What gave them the courage to overcome those barriers?

_____

_____

_____

_____

4. What most surprises you about Baptist history?

_____

_____

_____

_____

5. What have you learned from Baptist history that most challenges you? How can you confront those challenges?

_____

_____

_____

_____

6. In 1792, William Carey preached a sermon based on Isaiah 54:2-3. He concluded his sermon with this statement: "Expect great things—attempt great things." How have you and your church expected great things from God? How have you attempted great things for God?

_____

_____

_____

_____

Chapter 2

A Brief Introduction to Baptist Thought: What Do We Believe?

The history of Baptists shows how Baptists began over differences of belief and practice with prevailing custom. Baptists held their convictions strongly and deeply. They showed their commitment by their courage in the face of persecution. Occasionally, they also showed it by parting ways with fellow Baptists. Sometimes those divisions were peaceable. Sometimes they were not. Nevertheless, the result is an incredible variety of different kinds of Baptists in various areas of the world. What, then, makes one a Baptist?

It is important to understand that no one holds or owns a patent, a copyright, or a trademark on the term "Baptist." As we have seen and will explore further, Baptists are from the "free church" tradition. As a result, if some person, church, or group wants to claim the name, no one may prevent them.

However, certain doctrines have been at the heart of Baptist origins and history. We will look at five in this chapter: authority of Scripture, believer's baptism, priesthood of all believers, autonomy of the local church, and religious liberty and the separation of church and state. Sometimes we call these "Baptist distinctives." To do so is not to claim that we Baptists are the only ones who believe or practice these distinctives. Certainly, many other Christian denominations, groups, and churches also claim one or more of them.

The purpose of this chapter is to look at the five distinctives and see how Baptists formed as a group of people who believed in those ideas. What do the distinctives mean, and how have Baptists practiced them over the centuries? How do they make Baptists who they are? In this chapter, where appropriate, specific references will be made to the 1963 *Baptist Faith and*

Message. This document most closely reflects the historic Baptist views and faith regarding the areas of concern.

We will address them in an intentional order. They are all interwoven, and each influences and shapes all the others. Even so, the foundational distinctive is related to authority.

Authority of Scripture

Some of the most emotional disagreements among Baptists continue to involve our respective views and interpretations of the Bible. The bad news is that we are divided—despite Jesus' death to reconcile us not only to God, but also to each other (1 Cor 1; Eph 2:11-22; Eph 4; Col 3). What good news, then, can there be? Simply this: as long as we are arguing about the Bible, we are taking its authority seriously.

Authority. The word has many uses and implications. One thesaurus lists the following as synonyms for authority: power, right, ability, influence, weight, clout, last word (and the list goes on).

One context in which we see the use of authority is the military. What gives a superior the power, right, ability, or clout to give an order to soldiers and expect them to carry it out? Simply stated, it is the authority held by means of rank. Of course, even that power can be wielded only within the "chain of command." In the United States, that chain of command reaches up through the ranks to the president. Thus, the president is the "commander-in-chief" of the U.S. military. But even the president's authority is derived from elsewhere: the Constitution of the United States. Further, in its preamble, we see that even the authority of the Constitution comes from elsewhere: "We, the people." After all, we, the people of the United States, can—and sometimes do—change or amend the Constitution. So, ultimately, the citizens empower one soldier to command another to accomplish whatever purposes are deemed necessary. We can see similar examples in law enforcement, education, and the corporate world. In fact, seldom (if ever) does anyone function free from authority. There is always someone or something to tell us what to do, what not to do, or to give us boundaries. Sometimes we voluntarily submit to an authority, or it might be imposed.

History has shown that one of the greatest concerns of the early Baptists was that the church was doing and believing things that could not be found in the Bible. Clergy and councils had created the creeds and commanded the practices. The biggest problem was this: how could they be sure these beliefs and practices were of God? After all, it only seems proper that any belief about God and any practice to honor and obey God should come from God.

The answer is in the Bible itself. In 2 Timothy 3:16-17, Paul writes, "All Scripture is inspired by God and profitable for teaching, for reproof, for correction, for training in righteousness; so that the man of God may be adequate, equipped for every good work" (NASB).

However, Baptists do not believe the Bible is authoritative in and of itself. Rather, God's inspiration is at the root of Scriptural authority. What, then does "inspired" mean? Simply stated, it means "God-breathed." The Hebrew word *ruach* means both spirit and breath. The same is true of the Greek word *pneuma*. By saying that the Bible is inspired by God, Paul was stating God's direct involvement in its development and writing. Despite their differences, Baptists, by believing in the authority of Scripture, are referring to the authority of God. The Spirit of God, the Holy Spirit, formed and shaped Scripture. God breathed life and power into it.

Among Baptists, there are many different understandings of how God did that. The Bible is a product of God's partnership with humanity. We know from the Bible itself that God used people to write the Bible. We know the names of many, but other names we don't know. But they *were* people. They wrote through the lenses of their own experiences and cultures. They wrote through their own understandings of the structure of the universe. Further, according to the Bible, these humans whom God used to write the Scripture were flawed (Rom 3:23)! The same thing is true of people over the centuries whom God used to preserve and transmit the Bible. Is that to suggest that the Bible is flawed? By no means. Instead, it is to say that God's work did not end with the initial inspiration. Further, it serves as a demonstration of God's grace and power.

The 1963 *Baptist Faith and Message* calls the Bible "a record of God's revelation to man," stating that the Bible is "a perfect treasure of divine instruction." By affirming the authority of Scripture, Baptists are saying a lot about the Bible. They are taking most seriously Martin Luther's call for *sola scriptura* (Scripture alone). For Baptists, this means the Bible is the touchstone for all discussion regarding Christian faith and practice. If Jesus is our Lord, it makes sense that we should follow Jesus' instructions.

These instructions are not intended only for the people to whom its various books were addressed two millennia ago and more. Accepting the authority of Scripture means accepting that the Bible is relevant *today*. Again, we see God at work. Through God's grace, Scripture shows us our need for that grace and how to receive it. Through God's power, that ancient book speaks to our twenty-first-century world. That is what we can call "inspired"!

If we accept the Bible as authoritative for faith and practice, we have obligations. Let's look at a few.

First, if the Bible is authoritative, *it must be "open."* That means it must be available to everyone. In the past, the Bible was a closed book to many. Often this was because they were prevented from reading and studying it. The church and clergy read, interpreted, and applied the Bible for people. "Correct" doctrine was taught to them through the creeds the church and clergy developed. Many Christians were persecuted and even martyred for wanting the Bible to be in the languages and the hands of all Christians. We must not take their sacrifices for granted.

Second, *the Bible must be submitted to the Lordship of Christ.* The 1963 *Baptist Faith and Message* puts it this way: "The criterion by which the Bible is to be interpreted is Jesus Christ." This simple statement says a lot. It is a powerful theological statement about the Bible. It reminds us of the fullness of God's work in relation to Scripture. As Holy Spirit, God inspired the Bible. In like manner, as the Son, God illuminates our study and understanding of the Bible. God not only breathes life and power into Scripture. Through the Bible God has revealed Himself to us. What is even more wonderful is that God's work continues. God also wants to work in us to shed light on our study. Further, God empowers us to live as we are called.

Notice that there's a certain cycle implied here. When we accept Jesus as our Lord, we commit to obey Him. To discover His commands, we study the Bible He inspired. As we study the Bible, we need our Lord's help to understand how this ancient book applies to our lives today. The best example we have is the life of Jesus Himself. When we see how Jesus lived out the commands of God, we have a better idea of how we ought to live. What we learn often frightens us. We are mere human beings; we are weak. How can we live that way? The best way to find the answer is to look into the Bible again. In the Bible are many instances of God empowering people to do the impossible. Once again, the best example is Jesus Himself. Submission to the Lordship of Christ calls us to a study of the Bible. Then our study of the Bible calls us to continuing submission to the Lordship of Christ.

Third, *we must take the Bible seriously.* We might show this in many different ways. Some people read the Bible every day. Others never put anything on top of the Bible. Some might never write in their Bibles. Still others make numerous notations in their Bibles' margins.

Probably the best way to take the Bible seriously is to put its opinions above our own. We like to think we do this, but do we really? After all, it is difficult. Romans 3:23 reminds us that "all have sinned and fall short of the glory of God" (NASB). That means our sinful nature can influence even our Bible study. (And it makes submission to the Lordship of Christ all the more vital!) When we take the Bible seriously, we, not the Bible, are changed. When we take the Bible seriously, we are careful not to make it mean what we want it to mean. As a friend and colleague, the late Dr. William Hendricks, once said, "There is a difference between the authority of Scripture and the authority of anyone's interpretation of what the Bible says." This is why the authority of the Bible must supersede that of creeds and confessions and our own, individual opinions.

This is not to suggest that we should not be people of conviction. Rather, taking the Bible seriously means we must let it *always* continue to shape our Christian views and practices. When we take the Bible seriously, we will not remain the same. We will change and we will grow.

The fourth "must" is the result of the first three—*the Bible must be studied seriously*. Paul wrote to Timothy (in 2 Tim 2:15), "Be diligent to present yourself approved to God as a workman who does not need to be ashamed, accurately handling the word of truth" (NASB). When the Bible is open to us, when we submit it to the Lordship of Christ, and when we take it seriously, its study will become more vital to us. Perhaps you have seen cars sporting a bumper sticker that reads, "God said it. I believe it. That settles it." God said it, and that settles it—whether or not we believe it!

The point of Bible study is to discern more accurately and fully what God is saying. However, even the "simple" passages, when taken seriously, become more profound. For example, John 3:16 is a simple and wonderful statement of God's love for the world. Among Christians, it is probably the most memorized and quoted passage in the entire New Testament. Its simplicity has led many to accept God's love and commit to Jesus as Lord. That, indeed, is a wonderful thing. To take it seriously means to dig even more deeply into it. That is when we discover that God's love is for everyone. It is not just for us; it is for our family, for our friends, even for our enemies. A basic understanding of John 3:16 has to do with our individual relationships with God. A deeper study of the same passage has implications for all our relationships.

However, Bible study must go a step further. James 1:22 says, "But prove yourselves doers of the word, and not merely hearers who delude themselves" (NASB). This is the fifth "must" statement: *the Bible must be basis of personal religious experience.* That is, the Bible should shape our lifestyles as Christians. Just as the Holy Spirit was at work in the development of the Bible, so the Holy Spirit speaks to us, leads us, and empowers us through our study and reading of it. Further, this is consistent with God's purpose in breathing life into, or inspiring, the Bible: so that Christians will be "equipped for every good work" (2 Tim 3:17, NASB). Our "equipping" works at least three different ways. First, as God's people, our lives should be consistent with God's commands as found in the Bible. Second, we must interpret our religious experiences in light of Scripture and not the other way around. To do otherwise is dangerous, for it puts our experience above the Bible. Third, as we consistently read and study the Bible, our ears and hearts must be open and ready for God's voice.

Our personal religious experience is not lived out only as individuals. Rather, we join with other Christians as churches. Therefore, the Bible must be at the center of and the foundation for everything a Baptist church does. This is what we can call the church's lifestyle. The third section of this book examines how to live out what we learn from the Bible.

The Ordinances: Believer's Baptism and the Lord's Supper

As described in chapter one, the church out of which Baptists grew had sacraments. Sometimes that term is used for any ritual of a church. However, the sacraments were more than rituals. They were the means by which God brought His grace to effect in the lives of people. On the other hand, Baptists believe that there are two ordinances: baptism and the Lord's Supper. Strictly speaking, they are not sacraments. Rather, the ordinances are rituals that Baptists believe are commanded by Jesus in Scripture. They are not the means by which God sends His grace into our lives. Rather, they are important symbols and reminders of how we have already experienced God's grace.

Baptism

The first religious practice with which Baptists took issue is the one from which they get their name: baptism. We have seen how the early Baptists opposed infant baptism. They saw no biblical basis for the practice. Instead, they believed only believer's baptism was biblical.

Christians did not invent the ritual of baptism. In Judaism, it was and is known as *miqvah*, a ritual bath of cleansing. The following people took part in the ritual: women after giving birth (Lev 12), Nazarites as they completed their vows (Num 6), lepers as part of the process of being declared clean (Lev 14:9), priests as they prepared to lead in certain rites in the temple, and those who had converted to Judaism in order to identify with their new faith. In Matthew 3 we read that many came to John to be baptized as a sign of their repentance. Of course, the New Testament details many instances of people being baptized as a result of their conversion.

Practice of infant baptism is based on two doctrines: those of the sacraments and original sin. According to the doctrines, human beings inherit original sin from Adam and Eve. Children are born with the taint of this sin. It is important, therefore, that baptism cleanse children from that stain. Those who practice infant baptism also point to Acts 2:38-39 (among other Bible passages) to defend their practice.

The Meaning of Baptism among Baptists

To say that baptism is an ordinance and not a sacrament is not to diminish its importance. The 1963 *Baptist Faith and Message* states that baptism is "an act of obedience symbolizing the believer's faith in a crucified, buried, and risen Savior . . . ." Thus, it is an important act of obedience and a *vital* symbol. Let's look at these two dimensions of baptism.

We know from John 4:1-2 that, early in His ministry, Jesus authorized His disciples to baptize. In the "Great Commission" (Matt 28:18-20), Jesus closely connected baptism with discipleship. Many subsequent New Testament passages link repentance and baptism, but the latter is to be performed in the name of Jesus. That is, one first repents of sin and commits to Jesus as Lord. A first act of obedience is to do what Jesus commanded: be baptized. For Baptists, this is one reason why the individual being baptized must be a believer. Only someone who has the maturity and logical capacity to choose can truly repent and truly obey. Both are conscious choices.

Further, baptism is also a symbol and not only an act of obedience. It reminds participants and observers that Jesus died, was buried, and rose from the dead. It also demonstrates that the candidate identifies with Jesus. She or he has died to the old life and now lives a new life in Jesus Christ. For the believer, then, baptism is a symbol that serves as a witness to what Jesus has done. It is also a proclamation of his or her commitment to and identity with Jesus. Similarly, it identifies the believer with Jesus' body: the church. First Corinthians 12:13 makes this clear: "For by one Spirit we were all baptized into one body, whether Jews or Greeks, whether slaves or free, and we were all made to drink of one Spirit" (NASB).

The Mode of Baptism among Baptists

The method and means of baptism also became vitally important to Baptists. The earliest English Baptists baptized through effusion, or pouring. Almost certainly this was because the mode of effusion prevailed in the church out of which they came. It was all they had known.

Soon, however, Baptists became convinced that baptism should be by immersion. This, too, was due to what they felt the Bible taught. *Baptizo* is the Greek word from which we get the term "baptism." It means "to dip." In 2 Kings 5:14, the Septuagint (the Greek Old Testament) uses the word in the story of the leper Naaman. In that story, Elisha tells Naaman to wash seven times in the Jordan River in order to be cleansed of his leprosy.

Over the years, details regarding the mode of baptism caused splinter groups among Baptists. Even today, some believe the candidate should be immersed three times: once for the Father, once for the Son, and once for the Holy Spirit. Some believe baptism should only occur in running water. Others claim it should be done only outside—as it was in biblical days. In many Baptist churches, only the pastor may baptize, while in others any member of the church may do so.

Baptisms take place at various times in both regular and special worship services in Baptist churches. Sometimes people are baptized at the beginning of the service, sometimes later. Sometimes the baptism is the central part of the worship service toward which all other parts point. Ministers vary in how they perform a baptism and what they say during one. They also read different Scripture passages, and sometimes someone other than the pastor reads them. A baptism offers a wonderful opportunity to share with those in attendance the meaning of the baptism and its place in Baptist history and doctrine. It also offers the one being baptized a chance to share words of witness with the congregation.

I have seen baptisms performed by Baptists around the world: in creeks and rivers, in lakes and ponds, in the surf off beaches, in swimming pools, and in baptisteries. The one thing that unites them all is the conviction that only believers should be baptized, and only by immersion.

The Lord's Supper

Though disagreeing theologically on its meaning, most Christian churches celebrate something like the Lord's Supper. Some consider it a sacrament. Baptists consider it, like baptism, a symbolic observation that fulfills Jesus' command.

Matthew 26:26-35, Mark 14:12-21, and Luke 22:14-23 tell of Jesus' celebrating this meal with His disciples. These passages and 1 Corinthians 11:23-27 provide almost all the direct biblical bases for the Lord's Supper. The Lord's Supper originated with the Jewish Passover meal. The Passover itself was a feast initiated by God in Mosaic Law. Its purpose was to celebrate God's freeing the Israelites from their Egyptian bondage. There were various aspects of the celebration. Each was designed to help the Jews not only recall, but also relive and better understand the experiences of their ancestors. The Passover meal, or Seder, was the centerpiece of the festival. Held in the home, the Seder followed a closely prescribed order. Each step, prayer, and element had meaning. It was a rich ceremony and remains so in contemporary Jewish practice.

The biblical accounts of Jesus' Last Supper—and, so, the Lord's Supper—are probably snapshots of one specific aspect of the meal. They all focus on two particular elements significant for all Christians: the bread and the wine. The Passover Seder would have included these elements also. However, Jesus gave them new meaning. Just as He had broken bread to feed His disciples, so would His body be broken to sustain them. Likewise, the wine represented the blood He was about to shed for them. In Luke and in the Corinthian account, Jesus proclaims that, through these elements, there is a "new covenant." Jesus also gave the command to celebrate the same "in remembrance" of Him. In 1 Corinthians 11:26, Paul writes that observing the Lord's Supper is a way to "proclaim the Lord's death until He comes" (NASB).

What Scripture Teaches about the Lord's Supper

What do these Scriptures teach about the Lord's Supper? First, the Lord's Supper—as an ordinance like baptism—*is an act of obedience*. According to the Bible (and we have affirmed the authority of Scripture), Jesus commanded His disciples to do it. That includes us. But Jesus told us to do it for a purpose, which He describes in Scripture.

Second, the Lord's Supper *is an act of remembrance*. Each time we celebrate this wonderfully rich ritual, we reenact and remember Jesus' sacrifice.

Our lives today are full of distractions. Many elements of our culture call for our attention and loyalty. It is essential for us to pause and take time to remember that Jesus died for us and deserves all our devotion.

Third, the Lord's Supper *is an act of proclamation.* As a reenactment, the Lord's Supper not only reminds us of Jesus' sacrifice, it also tells others. It offers those who do not participate—regardless of age—to ask those of us who do to explain its meaning. What a wonderful way to open the door for us, Jesus' disciples, to tell the wonderfully good news of God's love for all!

Fourth, too important for us to take for granted, the Lord's Supper *should be an act of reflection.* Many rituals become so common that participants begin to go through the motions. It should not be so with the Lord's Supper. Obviously, it calls us to meditate upon God's love and Jesus' sacrifice. But there is more. In 1 Corinthians 11:28, we read that before and during the Lord's Supper we should examine our hearts. This is a call for us to look at the sin in our hearts—the sin that drove Jesus to the cross. Also, it is much like Jesus' command about sacrifice in Matthew 5:23-24. There Jesus teaches His disciples to reconcile with others so that they can approach the altar of sacrifice with pure hearts.

According to Paul, in Ephesians 2:13-14, Jesus' sacrifice had two purposes: to reconcile sinful human beings to God and to bring people together. The Lord's Supper *should be an act of communion.* What do we all hold in common? First, if Romans 3:23 and 6:23 are true, we are all sinners and stand in need of what Jesus did. Further, if John 3:16 is true, God's love and Jesus' sacrifice are for everyone. In the Lord's Supper we celebrate what all people in Christ's body share. No one of us is better than any other. God's love is not for one of us more than any other. So, as an act of communion, the Lord's Supper should be humbling. The account of the Last Supper in the Gospel of John is revealing at this point. Unlike the other Gospels and 1 Corinthians 11, John 13 does not give details of the supper itself. However, it tells us of something important that Jesus did and taught just before the meal. As an act of humility, Jesus washed his disciples' feet. In John 13:15, we read that Jesus taught them, "For I gave you an example that you also should do as I did to you" (NASB).

It is heartbreaking to see rancor and conflict tear apart so many churches and Christian fellowships. The inordinate pride that often causes division is a terrible witness. How can the world believe our testimony of a reconciling God when we, who claim to be His, refuse to be reconciled to one another? Nor is this poor witness something new. The shame of disunity also infected the Antioch church of the New Testament. In Galatians 2, Paul tells of even Peter's refusal to eat with Gentiles. Psalm 133 tells us how much better is the witness of communion among God's people! This is one more of the many things we gain through the meaningful celebration of the Lord's Supper.

How We Observe the Lord's Supper

Each Baptist church decides how and when to celebrate the Lord's Supper. Above, I addressed the Landmark Baptist practice of "closed communion," in which only members of that local church can participate. There remain some Baptist churches that invite only members of like-minded *Baptist* churches to share communion. Most other Baptist churches, however, see the Lord's Supper as being served at the Lord's table. Thus, all who have accepted Jesus as Lord are invited to participate.

Regarding the Lord's Supper, Baptist churches vary on several issues. It may be observed once a month, once a quarter, or once a year. Unfortunately, some churches seldom practice this vital ordinance. One often sees the Lord's Supper being celebrated on or before Christmas and Easter or as part of other important church events such as an anniversary or dedication. Usually, it takes place sometime during the conduct of a regular or special worship service. Where and when in the service varies widely from church to church and from event to event. Some churches allow only the pastor and deacons to lead and serve the Lord's Supper.

Even the elements that are used and how they are served can vary. Breads of many types (e.g., "communion wafers," crumbled crackers, whole or torn loaves) are commonly used. Usually, grape juice is served instead of wine, but some churches do serve wine. American sensibilities usually require that the juice be offered in individual communion cups, but some Baptist churches find ways to use the "common cup." Further, the elements are distributed in a variety of ways. The order in which the ordinance occurs, the words and prayers offered (and who says them), the songs sung—all offer a wonderful opportunity for each Baptist church to celebrate the Lord's Supper creatively and in ways that best meet its needs, nurture its members, and serve the purposes for which the Lord's Supper is intended.

The Priesthood of All Believers

The Bible is (or at least should be) the foundation for everything Baptists do. As we have already noted, James 1:22 calls us to "do" what God tells us through the Bible. Also, 2 Timothy 3:16-17 reminds us that ultimately, the Bible was inspired so that people will be "equipped for every good work" (NASB). This is a call to action manifested by the priesthood of all believers.

Biblical Roots of Priesthood of All Believers

The phrase "priesthood of believers" does not appear in the Bible. Of course, neither does the term "Trinity," and we certainly believe that God is Trinity (Father, Son, and Holy Spirit).

Nevertheless, the concept of the priesthood of all believers has strong and undeniable biblical roots. The first root grows out of Exodus 19:6. God led Israel out of Egypt. Now they were encamped at Mt. Sinai. God called Moses aside and told him to remind Israel of how He had delivered them and how they would be His special possession. Toward that end, God said Israel "'shall be to me a kingdom of priests and a holy nation. These are the words that you shall speak to the sons of Israel" (NASB). When Moses told Israel what God had said, the people answered, "All that the LORD has spoken we will do" (Exod 1:8, NASB).

Despite their response, God's call and challenge may have caught Israel by surprise. In their world, only certain special people were priests. The priest was the one with distinctive knowledge about whatever deity they worshiped. The priest also had a unique relationship with that deity and was the voice for the divine. Therefore, the priest intervened for the people with their god, taught them about their god, and led them in sacrifices to their god. To this point, God had spoken to Israel through Moses and Aaron. Surely, they may have thought, only Moses and Aaron would be *their* priests on behalf of the Lord. We know that God would later establish, through the Mosaic Law, the unique office of the priest who would serve in similar ways. In this passage, though, God calls them *all* to be priests. This may have been a second surprise for Israel: God freed them not only for the sake of living in liberty, but for the purpose of service. God had a mission for them.

Christians also base the idea of priesthood of all believers on New Testament references. How do people today respond when faced with great trials and tragedy? We often ask what we did wrong. Perhaps we think we are simply not being what we ought to be. The Christian church of the late first century faced great hardship. Persecution took many forms: personal, professional, and economic difficulties as well as imprisonment, torture, and execution. Our ancestors in the faith probably reacted very much as we do. First Peter was written to people in such a situation. In 2:4-8, the author reminds them (and us, when we are so tempted) that Jesus, too, was rejected, but became the foundation of God's building. They (and we) are the building stones. Then, in verse 9, Peter writes, "But you are a chosen race, a royal priesthood, a holy nation, a people for God's own possession, so that you may proclaim the excellencies of Him who has called you out of darkness into His marvelous light" (NASB).

What encouragement! Like Israel, they were saved for a purpose! And the New Testament reveals more of the same. Revelation 1:6 and 5:10 make similar statements. Each time, the priesthood of all believers is linked to the people of God being a *holy* people. Being holy means being set apart—special. The Bible is filled with references to God as holy. God is above all. God is unique. Likewise, God sets His people apart. God called us out of the world and into salvation and service. In grace, God not only saved us, but chose to make us partners in His great work of redemption.

This priesthood is not *of all people*. It is the priesthood *of all believers*. One's conversion is vital to the concept. The conscious decision that rises out of conviction is essential. At our conversion, we say God comes to live in us. Our decision to convert and to live the Christian life is very personal.

What, then, does "the priesthood of all believers" mean? What does it say about us? What does it allow us to do? What does it challenge us to do?

Special Rights of the Priesthood of All Believers

The rights we have as a holy and royal priesthood are based on something called "soul competency." E. Y. Mullins described soul competency this way: "Of course this means a competency under God, not a competency in the sense of human self-sufficiency. . . . [T]he competency of the soul in religion excludes at once all human interference . . . . [R]eligion is a personal matter between the soul and God."[1] For Mullins soul competency was the basis of what he called the "religious axiom," which he described as asserting "the inalienable right of every soul to deal with God for itself."[2]

Our first right, then, is direct access to God. First Timothy 2:5 and Hebrews 8:6, 9:15, and 12:25 remind us that only Jesus is the mediator or go-between for our relationship with God. It is that personal. Matthew 27:51, Mark 15:38, and Luke 23:45 record the dramatic tearing of the temple veil at the moment of Jesus' death on the cross. This curtain set apart the Holy of Holies not only from the rest of the temple, but from the rest of the world. Only the high priest could enter and only once a year—on the Day of Atonement. Jesus' death, however, was the final atoning sacrifice.

Since Jesus' death, nothing stands between us and God. Jesus made it possible for each person to go directly to God for forgiveness, redemption, and everything else salvation entails.

Further, like priests in Judaism and other ancient religions, we can go directly to God for leadership, guidance, and strength in our daily lives. Because Baptists have long believed in the authority of Scripture, direct access to God also means we have access to God's word. Our second right as a priest is to read and study the Bible. Direct access to the Bible does not mean we can read into it anything we want. After all, Romans 3:23 still applies to us. As much as we may work at a correct interpretation, we can err in our understanding of God's word. In Romans 7:13-21, the apostle Paul shares about his own struggle with the responsibility of rightly "[handling] the word of truth" as he describes the task in 2 Timothy 2:15. When studying the Bible, we have the privilege of seeking the leadership of the Holy Spirit to understand and apply its truth to our lives. We still make mistakes. We have our biases and continue to misunderstand the Holy Spirit. This is why we must never think of the priesthood of all believers as some kind of rugged individualism. We need each other. The term is the priesthood of *all* believers. Just as we each can and should read, study, and think for ourselves, so we need each other to share and test our understandings. Even then, however, we are ultimately responsible for our own study, beliefs, and actions.

Regarding these two rights, we must keep in mind something essential. Pastors and other ministerial leaders have a legitimate role in churches. God established the Israelite priesthood. Similarly, the New Testament tells us that God calls certain people to fill offices of leadership in today's churches. First Corinthians 12:28 and Ephesians 4:11, for example, make that apparent. However, Ephesians 4:12 also clarifies the purposes of those leaders: "for the equipping of the saints for the work of service, to the building up of the body of Christ" (NASB). Although many church members are not often "saintly," the term in that verse refers to all of us as Christians. As the priesthood, we are *all* called to serve. We are *all* called to build up the church, the body of Christ. The purpose of church leadership is to train, equip, and send out the members to do the work to which they are called. As we will continue to see, this multi-faceted task has many dimensions and implications.

Special Responsibilities of the Priesthood of All Believers

The rights examined above lead to the responsibilities of the priesthood. First, there is *the responsibility to be holy*. First Peter 2:9 calls Christians a "royal priesthood." God gives us that status as "joint heirs" with Jesus (Rom 8:17). However, we must remember that, as noted above, 1 Peter 2:9 also says we are to be holy. Peter quotes the challenge God gave His people in Leviticus 11:44 and 19:2: "You shall be holy, for I am holy" (NASB). We know that God has set us apart. Our responsibility, then, is to live that way. Holiness is an essential characteristic of God. Our holiness links us to God. Jesus, in Matthew 5:48, makes the same connection: "Therefore you are to be perfect, as your heavenly Father is perfect" (NASB). As my grandfather used to say, "Now, that is a tall order." We can argue that Romans 3:23 says it is impossible for us to be perfect and to be holy as God is holy. Nevertheless, we should aspire to and work toward the goal of holiness. As a holy priesthood, all Christians are called to lives that are different from the rest of the world. We are to hold a different set of values. We are to hold ourselves to a standard of values and behavior that distinguishes us from others. What are the world's standards regarding materialism, revenge, power, justice, anger, mercy, and selfishness? Ours should be different. And it is our duty to live by those holy standards.

Second, 1 Peter 2:9 indicates that we have *the responsibility to be on mission*. We are to "proclaim the excellencies" (NASB) of God. The Mosaic Law contains many detailed descriptions of the job of Israelite priests. In like manner, Jesus, in the Great Commission, summarizes our tasks as disciples and a priesthood: "Go therefore and make disciples of all the nations, baptizing them in the name of the Father and the Son and the Holy Spirit, teaching them to observe all that I commanded you; and lo, I am with you always, even to the end of the age" (NASB). As priests, our mission is to go, evangelize, and teach.

A third responsibility is *the responsibility for each other*. That is, we are priests to each other. Though we are saved as individuals, ours is not a faith of individualism. We need each other. We are to be available to support and encourage each other. As we have already seen, Ephesians 4:12 tells of the importance of Christians being equipped to build up the body of Christ. First Thessalonians 5:11 challenges us: "Therefore encourage one another and build up one another, just as you also are doing" (NASB). Someone truthfully observed, "Christians are the only army that shoots its wounded." Part of our responsibility is to hold each other accountable. Paul calls us to this mutual submission in Ephesians 5:21. However, we are also responsible for being a part of God's redemptive work. "To encourage" literally means to foster courage in another. We do this often at athletic events, cheering our favorite team even when the members make mistakes or fall behind. What if Christians treated each other this way? Even Christians make mistakes. Some are intentional. Others are inadvertent. Sometimes we may disagree on what is sinful. Still, we must remember that, other than holiness, there is another essential quality of God: mercy. In Luke 6:36, Jesus made a connection that is like the one He made to God's holiness: "Be merciful, just as your Father is merciful" (NASB). In Matthew 6:12 (in the "Lord's Prayer" or the "Model Prayer" as it is sometimes called), Jesus connects our forgiving others with our own forgiveness.

How, then, do we balance holding each other accountable and being merciful? Jesus gave a wonderful example when confronted with a woman caught in the act of adultery. John 8:11 records that, after the accusers had gone away, Jesus said to the woman, "I do not condemn you, either. Go. From now on sin no more" (NASB). Surely His words encouraged her. We should follow Jesus' example as we relate to one other.

In good times and bad, the world can weigh heavily on us. But aren't we called to be different? How much better would our lives be if we spent more time encouraging each other and less time joining the world in its assaults? We would certainly present a better example to the world and a more accurate testimony not only to God's holiness, but also to God's love and mercy.

Our fourth task is *the responsibility to serve*. This is among Jesus' most important teachings. The world says we should seek ever-greater personal power and use it for our own advancement. It tells us to "look out for number one" and suggests that all others are there for our service.

Not so with Jesus and His priesthood. In Matthew 20:26-28 He says, "It is not this way among you, but whoever wishes to become great among you shall be your servant, and whoever wishes to be first among you shall be your slave; just as the Son of Man did not come to be served, but to serve, and to give His life a ransom for many" (NASB). One example of such service is when Jesus washed the feet of His disciples. John 13:1-20 tells the story. In verse 14 we read of Jesus' command: "If I then, the Lord and the Teacher, washed your feet, you also ought to wash one another's feet" (NASB). In 1 Corinthians 12:25, Paul reminds us that the purpose of the gifts with which God entrusts us is to strengthen and unify believers and that Christians "should have the same care one for another" (NASB).

Why did you join your church? Was it to be served or to serve? Certainly, we sometimes need the service of others. This is the purpose of our priesthood: if all of us serve, we will all be served as needs arise. In Acts 2:44-45, the early church demonstrates reciprocal service.

The priesthood of all believers helps us understand our call both as individuals and as members of the community of faith and our particular churches. Each of us is to serve and be served, love and be loved, teach and be taught. We are servant priests to each other. One church bulletin expressed it well. Included in a list of church staff was the following line: "Ministers of the church: All the members of this church." This is what Baptists mean by the priesthood of all believers, and this is the way we should live and serve.

Local Church Autonomy

Above, I discuss how the priesthood of all believers should be lived out by individuals *in* a church. Local church autonomy is the way it is lived corporately *by* a church. Important to note at the outset is that belief in the autonomy of the local church does not deny the existence of the church universal. There are certainly Christians beyond the fellowship of Baptists. All the people of God—of all nations and all times—are and can rightly be called "the church." This doctrine relates to the freedom and function of the fellowship of believers as experienced and expressed in a local context. It is arguably the immediate and most visible expression of God's people.

The term "autonomy" simply means "self-government" or "independence." With all due respect, whenever I see a sign for an "independent Baptist church," I think to myself, "Well, of course! *All* Baptist churches are independent!" The 1963 *Baptist Faith and Message* puts it this way: "A New Testament church of the Lord Jesus Christ . . . is an autonomous body, operating through democratic processes under the Lordship of Jesus Christ. In such a congregation, members are equally responsible."

The Biblical Basis for Local Church Autonomy

The belief in local church autonomy begins with Jesus Christ as the head of any New Testament church. In Matthew 16:18, Jesus states clearly that the church was (and still is) *His*. Ephesians 4:15 and 5:23-24 and Colossians 1:18 attest to Jesus as the head of the church. Ephesians 5:25-26 gives the simple reason: Jesus bought and cleansed the church with His sacrifice. This is vital and logical. If, by Jesus' death, we are redeemed, then we belong to

Him. Therefore, a church is an association of reconciled believers. If we belong to Jesus individually, so we do together.

Local church autonomy is directly related to the priesthood of all believers. Soul competency and responsibility apply not only to us as individual Christians, but also to us as churches. Soul competency means each believer, under the leadership of the Holy Spirit, has the ability and right to interpret Scripture for himself or herself. The rights and responsibilities of the priesthood of all believers are rooted in individual freedom and service. Likewise, the church, the local body of believers, is rightfully self-governing, or autonomous, under God.

Early Baptists contended for local autonomy on the basis of their love for biblical doctrine. In 1611, as mentioned earlier, Thomas Helwys wrote that no officer of a church has authority over any other church or over any officers of other churches. The General Baptists followed this view. Two of the earliest Particular Baptist statements of faith, the *First London Confession* of 1644 and the *Second London Confession* of 1689, agreed.

The Freedom of Local Church Autonomy

Simply stated, local church autonomy means freedom of choice. Each church is free to choose how it will govern itself and how it will function. First, local church autonomy recognizes that *each church has the freedom to choose its leaders.* Most Baptist churches have similar types of officers. Among these are pastors, deacons, teachers, trustees, committees (and their chairpersons), and ushers, among others. Church members freely choose these officers. No human authority exists that can dictate those choices to churches. Rather, each church is free to make those decisions. Further, each church is free to decide the functions of each office and which persons they will select to hold the positions of responsibility. Of course, those choices are hopefully made after consideration of biblical teaching and under the leadership of the Holy Spirit. Does this mean all Baptist churches agree on the proper church offices? Is there consensus on how those offices should operate individually or together? Would every Baptist church agree with a given church's choices of the people who serve as its officers? Obviously, the answer to each of these is "no." This is why the autonomy of the local church is a call to respect as well as to freedom. As churches and individuals, we may wonder, disagree, and even shake our heads at the choices made by another church. But those choices are not ours to make. We must respect their freedom as we would want—and expect—them to respect and honor ours. This is consistent with the teaching of Jesus to "treat people the same way you want them to treat you" (Matt 7:12, NASB).

Local church autonomy also acknowledges that *each church has the freedom to choose how it will worship*. As we will see in an ensuing chapter, worship styles vary widely. Regardless of the style or form, our worship reflects that of first-century Judaism. Worship includes many elements, including (but not limited to) music, Scripture, prayer, leaders, and order. Personal and corporate preferences, traditions, and experiences influence each element. They are also shaped by diverse understandings of biblical teaching regarding worship. It is no surprise, then, that the ways in which a church may worship are almost limitless. Given all the possibilities, who can decide for a local church the best way for its people to worship? Who can decide the best worship by which a church will reach its community? How should the Bible shape the way a local church worships? Those decisions require an intimate knowledge of a particular church and its environment and, of course, the Bible. As mentioned above, one of the responsibilities of a priest was to lead worship. It follows logically that only the fellowship of priests—the local church—is equipped to make choices about worship. Autonomy of the local church requires that each church has both the right and the responsibility to do so. When a church prayerfully and thoughtfully makes biblically based choices regarding worship, that worship will become more vibrant, meaningful, life-changing, and empowering. It will genuinely belong to that church. It will be the true sacrifice of praise from the hearts of the church's people. Doesn't God, through the Bible, call us to that kind of worship? It *is* possible if each church exercises its freedom to choose its worship.

Thirdly, local church autonomy recognizes that *each church has the freedom to choose its ministries*. Every church is unique in the kinds of ministries it needs and is equipped to do. Think of the many ways in which communities, neighborhoods, cities, and towns can differ. For each difference, there are countless needs. A local church can feel overwhelmed. Fortunately, the Bible offers at least two great promises that should encourage us as we minister in God's name. First, in Exodus, God called Moses to lead Israel out of bondage in Egypt. The task overwhelmed Moses, and he was reluctant to go. However, in Exodus 3:12, God responds with a promise: "Certainly I will be with you" (NASB). We see similar examples throughout the Bible. Whenever God calls anyone to a job, God promises His presence. Jesus made that promise to us, His disciples, in the Great Commission: "and lo, I am with you always, even to the end of the age" (Matt 28:20, NASB).

The second promise is most obvious in some of the letters of Paul the Apostle. In 1 Corinthians 12, Paul makes it clear that God entrusts Christians with many different kinds of gifts to perform many different kinds of ministries. He makes the same observation in Romans 12:6 as does Peter in 1 Peter 4:10. God's promise is simply this: not only will God be with us, but He will equip us to do the tasks to which He calls us.

Again, who but the local church is in a better position to discern the needs of the community in which it resides? After all, God called the members of the church out of that very community! Further, who knows the gifts within a local church better than its members? Local church autonomy gives each church the right and the responsibility to discover the needs around it. Each church also has the right and responsibility to discover gifts God has entrusted to its members. We should not take these discoveries lightly. Neither needs nor gifts are always apparent. Discerning needs and how best to meet them is serious business. The same goes for recognizing and developing gifts for use in ministry. Both require prayer, study, and a deep desire for and openness to the leadership of the Holy Spirit. It is vital, then, that each church be entrusted to make its own decisions.

Finally, local church autonomy recognizes that *each church has the freedom to choose its associations*. This is the "flip side" of the independence granted each church by its autonomy. Above, I noted that the priesthood of all believers is not a call to isolated individualism. The same goes for autonomy of the local church. No church—regardless of size or situation—can do it all. Even the earliest English Baptists recognized this and joined with like-minded churches in associations. The same happened as Baptists came to North America.

Autonomous churches still need each other. Each is still free to cooperate with others. Each is free to choose *with whom it will cooperate*. Doctrine, moral and ethical issues, ethnicity, and geography influence that choice. One finds Baptist churches cooperating with other Baptist churches through local, state, national, and international groups known as associations, conventions, alliances, and fellowships. (The same is true with various other kinds of organizations with which a Baptist church may choose to cooperate). Each church's decision at this point is usually shaped by its answer to the matter of purpose. Churches may cooperate for the purpose of accomplishing a ministry or mission they cannot do alone, even in the local setting.

Churches may cooperate due to common interests or to exert influence they would not have alone.

Each organization may—and probably does—have certain membership expectations and requirements. However, within that framework, each church is free to decide for itself *how it will cooperate.* How will a church invest human and financial assets? It is a matter of stewardship, and stewardship is a matter of allotting the resources God has entrusted to us. Likewise, each church must decide why, how, and when to use finances and the time, energy, and talents of its members.

Some may observe that too much freedom can lead to chaos. However, the reverse may also be true—and possibly more likely. Anyone who has been involved in a church knows the level of disorder that sometimes takes place. Though of God and established and bought by Him, a church is made up of human beings. Romans 3:23 applies within all churches. Imagine the chaos if every church tried to be involved in every other church's business!

Local church autonomy has serious implications for each church. There is more to being a church than "just being a church." Church members have many choices to make. If a church is to follow the command of 1 Corinthians 14:40, preparation for making those decisions must include prayer, Bible study, and reflection. Those same elements of preparation must continue as a church acts on its decisions.

Local church autonomy means that, ultimately, each local church belongs to God, not to any human or human organization. Jesus is the head of any true church; that is our ideal as Baptists. It means freedom, but church members are not, under God, free to do as they please. Rather, local church autonomy calls each church and each of its members to take seriously the charge and responsibility as the body of Christ and to follow Him above all.

Religious Liberty/Separation of Church and State

Imagine what citizens in many countries experienced throughout history in places where church and state were not separate. You would have to observe the faith required by law. You would worship as the government dictated. You would be required to have your infants baptized and, later, taught in the state church. If you chose to defy the state and church, authorities would seize your property, imprison you and your family, and perhaps execute you.

Baptists have long taught and preached against such oppression. As a result, many of them died.

This final distinctive is both derived from and based on the others. It is the one most "distinctive" to Baptists. Arguably, it is the greatest contribution of Baptists to the history and governance of the United States. E. Y. Mullins referred to it as "Another Great Baptist Principle."[3] It is probably the most misunderstood and the most controversial. It is the Baptist belief in and call for religious liberty and the separation of church and state. The late George W. Truett, while pastor of First Baptist Church, Dallas, Texas, said, "Never, anywhere, in any clime, has a true Baptist been willing, for one minute, for the union of church and state, never for a moment."[4]

As we saw in the previous chapter, whenever the church and the government became entwined, persecution and intolerance resulted. As Truett was apparently aware, from their beginning, Baptists opposed the intermingling of church and state. John Smyth, in *Propositions and Conclusions concerning True Christian Religion, containing a Confession of Faith of certain English people, living in Amsterdam* (1612), wrote,

> the magistrate is not by virtue of his office to meddle with religion, or matters of conscience, to force or compel men to this or that form of religion, or doctrine: but to leave Christian religion free, to every man's conscience, and to handle only civil transgressions (Rom. xiii), injuries and wrongs of man against man, in murder, adultery, theft, etc., for Christ only is the king, and law giver of the church and conscience.[5]

Smyth's contemporary, Thomas Helwys, wrote in *A Short History of the Mystery of Iniquity* that through Romans 13:1-3 "has God given our lord the king all worldly power which extends to all the goods and bodies of his servants."[6] However, Helwys continued, "neither has our lord the king by that sword of justice power over his subject's consciences."[7] Later, in North America, Roger Williams agreed regarding the same passage.[8] As a result, he wrote that "all civil states, with their officers of justice, in their respective constitutions and administrations are proved essentially civil, and therefore not judges, governors, or defenders of the spiritual, or Christian, state and worship."[9]

John Leland was among the many subsequent Baptist leaders in the United States who continued this tradition. Leland influenced the views on religious liberty and church–state separation held by both Thomas Jefferson and James Madison and, therefore, influenced the U.S. Constitution.

Baptists were among those who pressured for the Bill of Rights to be added to the Constitution. Of course, the Bill of Rights includes the First Amendment and its statement, "Congress shall make no law respecting an establishment of religion, or prohibiting the free exercise thereof." The Danbury, Connecticut, association of Baptists was concerned that the (then) new Constitution should have a *strong* statement about separation of church and state, an important Baptist belief. They wrote Thomas Jefferson seeking reassurance. It was in Jefferson's response to the Danbury Baptist Association that he wrote this well-known statement: "I contemplate with sovereign reverence that act of the whole American people which declared that their legislature should 'make no law respecting an establishment of religion, or prohibiting the free exercise thereof,' thus building a wall of separation between Church and State."[10]

In 1920, George Truett connected Jesus' statement in Matthew 22:21 with this Baptist principle: "That utterance of Jesus 'Render unto Caesar the things that are Caesar's, and unto God the things that are God's,' is one of the most revolutionary and history-making utterances that ever fell from those lips divine. That utterance, once for all, marked the divorcement of church and state."[11]

Implications of Religious Liberty and the Separation of Church and State

Of course, how to understand and apply that statement and the First Amendment is a complex and often controversial matter. That is of concern to us, but it's not the issue here. Rather, we need to examine the consequences of religious liberty and church–state separation for us as individuals and churches today. For both the church and state, it has to do with authority and freedom. To be consistent with Matthew 22:21, there are two sides: Caesar's (the state) and God's (the church).

Religious liberty and the separation of church and state recognize the rightful authority and responsibilities of each entity. The earliest English Baptists, John Smyth and Thomas Helwys, clearly differentiated between the rightful authority of the state and that of the church. Roger Williams expressed it this way: "the church of Christ does not use the arm of secular power to compel men to the faith or the profession of the truth, for this is to be done by spiritual weapons, whereby Christians are to be exhorted, not compelled."[12]

E. Y. Mullins described it well:

The direct allegiance in the Church is to God, in the State it is to law and government. One is for the protection of life and property, the other for the promotion of spiritual life. An established religion, moreover, subverts the principle of equal rights and equal privileges to all which is part of our organic law. Both on its political and on its religious side the doctrine of separation of Church and State holds good.[13]

Mullins was not suggesting that civil governments were necessarily evil. Rather, the authority of any government appropriately relates to the secular. This is consistent with Romans 13:1-3. Whenever a government inserts itself in spiritual affairs, it oversteps its authority. Rather, Baptists say, God, as revealed through the Bible, is the authority in spiritual matters. Not the government. Not even the majority.

Our belief and the biblical doctrine is not "the priesthood of the government" or "priesthood of the majority." The responsibility of the state is not to do the work of the church. In Ephesians 6:12, the Apostle Paul contrasted the concern and work of the church with that of civil government: "For our struggle is not against flesh and blood, but against the rulers, against the powers, against the world forces of this darkness, against the spiritual forces of wickedness in the heavenly places" (NASB). The call of the church is for the church and not for the state. Jesus' Great Commission was given to His disciples and not to any government.

Religious liberty and the separation of church and state recognize the rightful freedoms of all. Mullins described the ideal as "a free church in a free state."[14] For the state this means freedom to function in and for justice on behalf of *all* its citizens. The government can do its work unencumbered by religious biases that, history shows, inevitably lead to spiritual oppression and coercion.

George W. Truett described the doctrine of biblical authority as foundational to the priesthood of all believers and to religious liberty. For the Bible to be one's "rule of faith and practice," Truett said, one must be free from externally imposed traditions, customs, councils, confessions, and ecclesiastical formulations. Only then can people live "simply and solely [by] the will of Christ as they find it revealed in the New Testament."[15]

Religious liberty is often expressed as "freedom *of* worship." Indeed, it is that. But it is much more. It is the freedom *to* worship *where*, *when*, and *how* we please. It also means neither we nor any other citizen should be coerced or pressured into worship. We are free to have a truly personal religion. We have chosen it. It is something we believe, and our worship is from our hearts. Stressing the absolute necessity for religion to be personal, Truett observed that "God wants free worshippers and no other kind."[16] The same can be said related to Christians' tasks of evangelism, teaching, and service. God wants all our offerings to Him—our lives, hearts, energies, and time—to be voluntary, not coerced.

However, there are limits to our freedom. Galatians 5:13 expresses them this way: "For you were called to freedom, brethren; only do not turn your freedom into an opportunity for the flesh, but through love serve one another" (NASB). As is true with any of our freedoms, we each must remember not only ours, but also those of others. The separation of church and state extends religious liberty to all and not to a select few. The "Golden Rule" challenges Christians to put the freedoms of others before our own. First Corinthians 10:29-33 calls us to do the same.

Legally, our freedoms are limited in that they cannot infringe on those of others. (For example, the right to free speech does not mean one can yell, "Fire!" in a theater where there is no fire.) In living out religious liberty, each person must keep in mind the rights and safety of others. E. Y. Mullins acknowledged this when he wrote, "As to the Bible in public schools there has been much difference of opinion among Americans. Baptists very generally and consistently oppose the reading of the Bible in the schools, because they respect the consciences of all others."[17]

This does not deny the right and responsibility of Christians to live, work, and serve as citizens. As previously noted, figuring out the balance is often complicated. Religious liberty and the separation of church and state do not prohibit Christians from being involved in government. Nor do they call Christians to abstain from political processes. They do, though, bar church and state from entanglements that limit the freedom of *anyone* regarding religion. Baptists today owe it to their forebears to continue this vital part of their legacy.

Notes

[1] Edgar Young Mullins, *The Axioms of Religion* (Philadelphia: American Baptist Publication Society, 1908), 53–54.

[2] Ibid., 92.

[3] Ibid., 188.

[4] George W. Truett, *God's Call to America*, ed. J. B. Cranfill (Nashville: The Sunday School Board of the Southern Baptist Convention, 1923), 43.

[5] From William L. Lumpkin, *Baptist Confessions of Faith* (Philadelphia: Judson Press, 1959), 140.

[6] Thomas Helwys, *A Short History of the Mystery of Iniquity* (1611/1612), ed. Richard Groves (Macon GA: Mercer University Press, 1998), 33.

[7] Ibid., 35.

[8] Roger Williams, *The Bloudy Tenent of Persecution, for Cause of Conscience discussed in a conference between Truth and Peace*, ed. Richard Groves (Macon GA: Mercer University Press, 2001), 22.

[9] Ibid., 3.

[10] Thomas Jefferson, *Writings of Thomas Jefferson*, vol. 16, ed. Albert Ellery Bergh (Washington DC: Thomas Jefferson Memorial Association, 1905), 281–82.

[11] Truett, *God's Call*, 43.

[12] Williams, *Bloudy Tenent*, 25.

[13] Mullins, *Axioms*, 196.

[14] Ibid., 199.

[15] Truett, *God's Call*, 35.

[16] Ibid., 33.

[17] Mullins, *Axioms*, 197.

Study Questions

Read each of the Scripture passages listed below. Beside each, write the Baptist distinctive it most directly addresses.

• 1 Corinthians 11:23-27 _____

• 1 Corinthians 12:13 _____

• 1 Peter 2:4-9 _____

• 2 Timothy 3:14-17 _____

• Colossians 1:18 _____

• Matthew 22:15-22 _____

Answer these questions related to each of the Baptist distinctives.

A. *Authority of Scripture*

1. What does Hebrews 12:1-3 suggest about Jesus' role in shaping our understanding of the Bible?

_____

_____

_____

_____

2. What caution might Romans 3:23 give us regarding our interpretation of the Bible?

_____

_____

_____

3. What biblical teaching most challenges you?

_____

_____

_____

_____

4. What are some ways you can show you are submitted to the authority of the Bible?

_____

_____

_____

_____

5. How would you describe the various meanings and expressions of authority in daily life? How do you compare these to the Bible as our authority?

_____

_____

_____

_____

6. Is there a hymn that expresses what "biblical authority" means to you? Explain.

_____

_____

_____

_____

7. How did recognizing the authority of Scripture give rise to the Baptist denomination?

_____

_____

_____

_____

8. How has recognizing the authority of Scripture shaped Baptist beliefs?

_____

_____

_____

_____

B. Baptism

1. What do you think about when you watch a baptism?

_____

_____

_____

_____

2. How does the way a baptism is done teach about its meaning?

_____

_____

_____

_____

3. What were some steps toward current Baptist beliefs regarding baptism?

_____

_____

_____

_____

4. What do you recall of your own baptism? Consider sharing your experience with the class.

_____

_____

_____

_____

5. Is there a hymn that expresses what baptism means to you? Explain.

_____

_____

_____

_____

6. How does your church help make baptism meaningful? How could it make baptism even more meaningful?

_____

_____

_____

_____

C. *Lord's Supper*
1. What do you think about when you participate in the Lord's Supper?

_____

_____

_____

_____

2. What do you do to prepare for the Lord's Supper? What can you do to be better prepared?

_____

_____

_____

_____

3. Compare the meaning of the Lord's Supper to that of the Passover meal
   after which it is modeled. How are they alike? How are they different?

_____

_____

_____

_____

4. Is there a hymn that expresses what the Lord's Supper means to you?
   Explain.

_____

_____

_____

_____

5. How does your church help make the Lord's Supper meaningful? What
   are other ways it could make the Lord's Supper even more meaningful?

_____

_____

_____

_____

D. Priesthood of All Believers
1. Why is this distinctive known as "the priesthood of all believers" and not
   "the priesthood of all people"?

_____

_____

_____

2. How would you describe the two sides (rights and responsibilities) of the priesthood of all believers?

_____

_____

_____

_____

3. What rights do we have in the priesthood of all believers?

_____

_____

_____

4. What responsibilities do we find in the priesthood of all believers?

_____

_____

_____

5. What do you do to exercise the rights of your priesthood?

_____

_____

_____

_____

6. What do you do to exercise the responsibilities of your priesthood?

_____

_____

_____

7. Is there a hymn that expresses what "the priesthood of all believers" means to you? Explain.

_____

_____

_____

_____

8. How does your church encourage the priesthood of all believers among its members? What other ways could this Baptist distinctive be implemented in your church?

_____

_____

_____

_____

E. Autonomy of the Local Church
1. How does your church exercise its autonomy?

_____

_____

_____

_____

2. How do you and your church submit to Jesus as the head of the church?

_____

_____

_____

_____

3. What are your responsibilities as a member of your church as it exercises
   its autonomy?

_____

_____

_____

_____

4. How does autonomy of the local church relate to the priesthood of all
   believers?

_____

_____

_____

_____

5. Describe the ways your church cooperates with other churches.

_____

_____

_____

_____

6. How can/does your church act autonomously and still cooperate with other churches?

_____

_____

_____

7. What are your responsibilities as a member of your church as it cooperates with other churches?

_____

_____

_____

_____

8. Is there a hymn that expresses what the autonomy of the local church means to you? Explain.

_____

_____

_____

_____

F. Religious Liberty and Separation of Church and State
1. What are some dangers of church and state being intertwined? What are some historical examples?

_____

_____

_____

_____

2. Who were some early Baptists who spoke out for separation of church and
   state? Why was that important to them?

   _____

   _____

   _____

   _____

3. How does the Golden Rule (Matt 7:21; Luke 6:31) relate to religious
   liberty and the separation of church and state?

   _____

   _____

   _____

   _____

4. What is the difference between separation of church and state and
   separation of Christians and state?

   _____

   _____

   _____

   _____

5. What freedoms do we find when church and state are separate?

   _____

   _____

   _____

   _____

6. How does religious liberty and separation of church and state help us better understand and focus on our responsibilities as Christians? How does it help us better understand how we can recognize and respect the religious rights of others?

_____

_____

_____

_____

7. As Christians, what are our civic responsibilities?

_____

_____

_____

_____

8. Is there a hymn that expresses what religious liberty and separation of church and state mean to you? Explain.

_____

_____

_____

_____

Chapter 3

Building a Distinctively Baptist Church through Worship

When one hears the word "church," often the first image that comes to mind is the building. The church, of course, is much more than a building. It is *the people*—the members. When one pictures the people, usually the first image that comes to mind is that of the church joined together in worship. Worship is probably the most visible action a church does. To examine the influence of Baptist doctrines on churches, we will first focus on worship. What is worship? What role does it play in the lives of believers? How can a church worship in ways that build on and reflect Baptist distinctives?

What Is Worship?

Worship is usually described and defined in terms of praise, adoration, reverence, veneration. Various Greek words are translated "worship" in the New Testament. Their implications vary. They can refer to serving, paying homage, acting piously, and honoring.

Think of the word "worship." Divide it into two syllables: "wor" and "ship." "Worship" comes from an Anglo-Saxon word that literally meant "worth-ship." That is, it described that which was worthy or deserving of something.

We worship many different things. The point of this chapter, of course, is our worship of God. Further, since we Baptists consider the Bible authoritative in matters of faith and practice, and since worship relates to both, the foundation for our worship of God is the Bible.

In both the Old and New Testament, we read that God alone is worthy of praise, homage, and service. We are to worship God alone. The effect of the first commandment, in Exodus 20:3, is to worship God only. The "greatest commandment," in Deuteronomy 6:5, is a call to invest all of our being in loving and honoring God. The prayer of David in 1 Chronicles 29:10-18 tells why he thought God was worthy of honor. As a book of hymns, the focus of Psalms is worship. When tempted to worship Satan, Jesus responded that we are to worship God alone (Matt 4:10).

We will explore two examples of heavenly worship recorded in the Bible. The first is found in Isaiah 6:1-8. Verses 1-4 are filled with images and symbols revealing God's character. They tell of God's majesty, greatness, and glory. The cries of "holy, holy, holy" by the seraphim remind us of God's uniqueness as Creator, Sustainer, and Redeemer. Upon realizing the reality of all God is, Isaiah learned something. He became aware of the reality of who he and Israel were—especially in comparison to God. Isaiah realized that he was a "man of unclean lips." Israel was also unclean. They were all sinners. Then, with a burning coal, Isaiah's lips were purified.

However, the worship did not stop with Isaiah's realization of his and Israel's sinful condition or with the cleansing of Isaiah's lips. He heard God's call for someone to "go." Having seen the magnificence and glory of God, Isaiah excitedly offered all he had to give. Giving himself, Isaiah cried out, "Here am I. Send me!" (NASB).

This account of Isaiah's worship and call teaches us that in true worship, we see God for who God really is. As a result, we see ourselves for who we really are—sinners. In and through worship, God offers cleansing that only God can provide. However, just as Israel was brought out of Egypt to serve God, we are cleansed and saved for a purpose. When we truly worship, we not only see God, but our hearts and minds are tuned to hear His call. That call may take varying forms and may lead us to many different places.

The second biblical account of heavenly worship is found in Revelation 5–6. John sees a vision of Jesus, the Lamb of God. Throughout the passage, Jesus is repeatedly named as the only one worthy of worship. The reasons are similar to those presented in Isaiah's vision: Jesus reigns in majesty from His heavenly throne. But there is more. In Revelation 4:10, the twenty-four elders throw down their "golden crowns" in homage at the feet of the Lamb. In 5:9, these same elders sing of the reason for their reverence: Jesus' purchase of all humanity through the shedding of His blood. The result of this worship is more worship. The elders again, in 5:14, "fell down and worshipped." When we recall all that Jesus has done for us, how can we do anything but praise Him?

The first thing to remember about worship, then, is that it is directed God-ward. God is the "audience." We are the "performers" as individuals and together, as churches and congregations. Whatever the occasion, style, or form of worship, it should draw us closer to God and point others toward God.

Second, we can and should worship God through rituals or services of worship. For most of us, such formal gatherings immediately come to mind when we think of worship. Much of the Mosaic Law—recorded in Exodus, Leviticus, Numbers, and Deuteronomy—is directed to various forms of worship. Occasions for worship included many types of sacrifices, feasts, festivals, rituals of cleansing, and others. Whatever the purpose or form of the worship service, it is to be a celebration of God and God's character and activity.

Unfortunately, many churches are strongly divided over the issue of styles incorporated into their worship services. These disagreements are usually over the tension between "traditional" versus "contemporary" approaches to worship. I find this strange and distressing because both traditional and contemporary elements are derived from the same roots: Hebrew/Jewish worship.

Synagogue worship in the first century AD most directly influenced Christian worship as we know it today—regardless of style. Synagogue worship on the Sabbath included various kinds of prayers, Scripture reading, and explanation of and/or teaching about the Scripture. The reasons we still follow this format today are simple. Jesus was Jewish and worshiped in synagogues. Jesus' disciples and almost all the earliest Christians were Jewish. The first Christian sermon, recorded in Acts 2:14-41, was given at the Jewish temple. A Jew (Peter) preached it and based it on Jewish Scripture (Joel 2). It referred to Jewish issues. Further, Paul went first to the synagogues wherever he visited. (Even special times of worship today, such as the ordinances, weddings, funerals, and dedications reflect Jewish roots.)

What helps us worship today? Certainly, we sing songs and hymns that serve many purposes. They remind us of God's wonder and works. They are our witness. And we learn from them. Similarly, our prayers have varying purposes. Through them we converse with our God. They offer opportunities for confession, praise, and commitment. But conversation is a two-way street. Through our prayers and through meditation, we listen to what God says to us. The music in worship also affords us occasion for reflection. In the King James Version of the Bible, Psalm 46:10 is translated "Be still and know that I am God." The New American Standard Bible translates it

"Cease striving." In both translations, the call is to quiet one's heart to reflect and to hear the voice of God.

Bible reading is also a vital part of worship, whether an individual reads directly from Scripture or the congregation reads it aloud together. God speaks to us through the written word, and it aids our worship in every sense. The more we know about God through the Bible, the more reasons we find to worship. The sermon and other explanations and comments on the Bible reading are like the teaching in synagogue worship. They are meant to help us learn to apply the Bible to our lives and suggest how we can respond to the Bible's truth.

Offering and invitation are often parts of our worship, as they should be. Like the sacrifices of the Jewish temple, they require of us a certain commitment. It is one thing to praise God with our mouths. It is another to honor God with our possessions and with our lives.

Worship in the Lives of Believers and a Church

Worship is ultimately about relationship. In any growing, healthy relationship, there is increased intimacy. That is, those involved want to know more about each other. They work to make that happen. As Christians—living in a personal relationship with Jesus—we want to know more about God. As Jesus' body, we also want to know more about each other, God's world, and ourselves. As we understand more about who God is, we naturally discover more about who we are. We become more mindful of our total dependence on God. Worship is an opportunity for witness, submission, sacrifice, commitment, comfort, growth, and learning.

In worship we can find and experience what Robert Pazmiño calls five core Christian values: truth (the call to integrity), love (the call to care), faith (the call to action), hope (the call to courage), and joy (the call to celebration).[1] What, then, must we bring to our worship? Perhaps our most important contribution to worship is a heart willing to accept the truth, willing to love, willing to follow in faith, willing to hope, and willing to overflow with joy; a heart grateful that—in Jesus—we can dare to be willing; a heart open to and listening for God's voice.

With hearts like this, our worship will not become simply ceremonial. Rather, it will become much more personal. In our reverence for God, we should never resort simply to going through the motions. Adoration of Jesus includes emotions but should not be based on emotions alone. Genuine worship should lead to deeper self-evaluation through genuine confession that relies fully on God's love and grace. Deeper worship also leads to more profound dialogue with God as we share with and listen to God. We gain a greater recognition of Jesus alone as being deserving of all we have and are. Then, as both conviction and faith grow, we respond to God with words, songs, and the offerings of our lives and resources. Worship actually challenges the imagination. Like Isaiah (in Isa 6:1-8), we are able to see not only reality, but also the new possibilities God promises. Worship is a matter of experiencing two feelings that may seem contradictory. One is the grief when we realize the depth and cost of our sin. The other is the joy found in redemption. But the two need not contradict each other. In Jesus they complement and lead to each other. That is, the more our sin genuinely disturbs and grieves us, the more joy we find in experiencing God's grace.

As a church worships, it builds community with God and others. Worship can transform the entire church body as well as the individuals that make up that body. Thus, it is vital for a church to teach its people how to worship (together and separately). Then they can truly share the conviction, the grace, and the vision that are found in worship. Corporate worship should draw people together and into participation, unity, and mutual appreciation and support. The divisions mentioned in the earlier part of this section are distressing and saddening because that which was designed to unite Christians becomes a wedge to drive them apart.

Worship happens in service as well as in "services" of worship. The Apostle Paul, in Romans 12:1, called the Roman Christians to "present [their] bodies [as] a living and holy sacrifice, acceptable to God, which is [their] spiritual service of worship" (NASB). In a subsequent chapter, I discuss how Baptist doctrine should shape our lives of service. The point here is that nearly everything we can say about a worship service also holds true for our work as Christians. Above all, our service, too, is a celebration of God and God's character and activity. Ultimately, it is powered by God's Spirit and should point all of us God-ward.

Baptist Distinctives and Worship

What, then, can Baptist distinctives offer our worship as churches and individuals? How can we build our worship on these distinctives?

The Authority of Scripture

First, the Bible must define and guide our worship. The Bible must form and inform worship in a truly Baptist church. The structure, elements, and practices of our worship must conform to biblical precepts. (Notice that we do not practice infant baptism because, though baptism is an act of worship, infant baptism is not specifically advocated in the Bible.) Our worship should reflect that of the Bible—in character and purpose at least—while still speaking to our day and time. We can do this creatively and meaningfully through reading, singing, dramatizing, praying, and the many other elements we typically experience in worship. The following are a few examples.

Unfortunately, we sometimes rush through our Bible reading. Occasionally we even rush as we quote Bible passages. Maybe subconsciously we think that the more rapidly we can say it, the better we know it. It seems to me that the better we want to *know* and *experience* it, the more we need to slow down. If we hold to the authority of the Bible, we should savor it. It is not, then, simply a matter of *whether* we read the Bible, but also *how* we read it.

If the Bible is the foundation of our worship, its reading must be central. Romans 12:2 relates spiritual worship to being "transformed." As you may know, the Greek word translated "transform" is the origin of the term "metamorphosis." Metamorphosis happens when a caterpillar changes into a moth or a butterfly. What a difference! Since we belong to God, the changes worship brings in our lives should make us more godly or Christ-like. Through the Bible, God shows us how we should live.

The Bible must be the basis of our prayers. As with Bible reading, it is both a matter of *what* and *how* we pray. The diverse prayers of people appear throughout the Bible. Some focus on confession. Others seek God's guidance or comfort. There are also prayers of commitment, submission, and faith. Certainly, there are prayers for blessing, healing, and deliverance. There are also examples of how *not* to pray (Matt 6:5-8; Luke 18:11-12). Then, there is the "Lord's Prayer" or "Model Prayer" found in Matthew 6:9-13 and Luke 11:2-4. In those passages, Jesus models a prayer that centers completely on God's will. God's will was also at the heart of Jesus' prayer in the Garden of Gethsemane (Matt 26:39; Mark 14:36; Luke 22:42).

Our hymns often teach us more than we realize. Thus, the songs we sing should be consistent with the Bible. Yet, how often do we think about the words we sing and hold them up to the light of the Bible? How often do we focus more on our musical tastes? Many divisions related to worship occur in this area. Each of us naturally has personal preferences regarding music. The problem—for any of us—is when we let our partiality supersede the purpose of worship. Always insisting on our own way violates how the Bible teaches us to act (Matt 7:12; Luke 6:31; 1 Cor 13:5).

The Priesthood of All Believers

This vital Baptist doctrine calls us to examine both corporate and individual worship. As we worship together, we should see ourselves as leaders. This applies in two ways. First, the essence of worship is that we are all the "performers." If worship is directed God-ward, God is the audience. Second, if all believers are priests, the laity, not merely the ministers, should be involved in leading worship. If only the ministers lead in a worship service, they function as "high priests"—a concept alien to Baptist doctrine. Certainly, the pastor and other ministers have significant roles in worship leadership. They do not, however, have the only roles in leading worship. If the priesthood of all believers is practiced, the congregation should never be marginalized. Rather, the entire congregation, ministers and laity alike, are integral to worship. We should see our worship as a witness to each other—a sacrifice—involving the whole body of believers. This already happens many ways and in many churches. When a congregation sings, prays, and reads the Bible together, they put this doctrine into practice. There are many other ways, too, such as testimonies, choral and instrumental music, and dramas. Some pastors lead and train their laity to lead in worship through preaching from time to time. One pastor, for example, recognizes and encourages the priesthood of all believers by asking at the end of evening services, "Does anyone here have a sense of God's direction for our church and worship that they would like to share with us?"

Two keys to the exercise of the priesthood of all believers are *leadership* and *training*. One of the most exciting ministry experiences of a pastor is training the laity of the church to do the work of the church (Eph 4:12). But it must go further—the laity must be *released* and *encouraged* to do their work as a fellowship of priests.

The invitation is fundamental to the function of the priesthood. It is, first, an evangelistic moment inviting people to join the priesthood. It is also a time for the believers/priests to offer their sacrifices to God.

Everything I have written about a church worshiping together also applies to how we worship as individual Christians. If the individual priests are to grow spiritually, they must worship as individuals. Yet, many believers take no time to do so. Perhaps they do not know how. They may not be aware of their need and what they can gain from it. Here again is an opportunity for a church to lead, train, and encourage its members to function and grow as part of the priesthood.

The Autonomy of the Local Church

For effective church worship, each local body of believers must decide for itself how to worship. As a time of drawing together as one, worship is more effective when the church makes its own worship decisions. The individual church is in the best position to know what structures, forms, styles, elements, and leaders best serve its situation. Directions and instructions regarding the methods of each church are not given from someone else. Rather, autonomy grants the church "ownership" of its worship. It is well known that people involve themselves more deeply in events, organizations, and activities in which they feel a sense of investment.

We have seen how the church is a body of those "called out" from the world and from the local community in which they live and function. Worship is one of many ways a local church can witness to the community around it. The church formed of individuals from that local community can, through worship, express God through who they and their communities are. For that to happen, the individual church must be free to shape and conduct its worship in ways accessible to its community. Because, in Baptist life at least, each church is autonomous, each church selects the worship leaders, times, forms, music, and language that best meet its needs and those of its community.

This freedom carries with it tremendous responsibility for the church. Every church should take seriously the need to understand better its community and the people who live in it. Usually, that means discovering the diversity as well as the similarities that characterize most neighborhoods, towns, and communities. Then, armed with this awareness, the church can design worship that will attract and make sense to its people. This requires a lot of work, but it is worth the effort. It means being more deliberate and intentional in worship, not simply copying what we see on television or hear that other churches are doing. When we resort to following blindly the ways of others, we lose our freedom and independence.

The Ordinances of Baptism and the Lord's Supper

Viewing the ordinances as symbols rather than sacraments does not diminish their importance to worship. Both baptism and the Lord's Supper serve the purposes of witness and unifying the people of God. They remind worshipers of God's grace and great work of salvation. These are among the reasons why God is worthy of the honor we offer through worship.

Time and again, baptism and the Lord's Supper emphasize what the members of the church share: one Lord, one baptism. That makes them truly one body. Also, both baptism and the Lord's Supper are a witness to those who do not share in the experience of salvation. They are like plays or pageants that reenact the gospel. Therefore, the ordinances should be vital parts of our worship and not merely appended. We should never take them for granted, forget them, or ignore them. They are simply too important in our worship.

Religious Liberty and the Separation of Church and State

In many countries and at many times, civil states imposed worship on their people. The government was so influenced by one church or religion that it dictated when, where, and how all its citizens would worship.

However, Baptists recognized that the state, ultimately, has no power over the consciences of people. Worship is such a personal matter that a church, much less a government, cannot dictate it. When states have tried to do so, the inevitable results were not only loss of freedom but also loss of true worship. That is, the honor and praise became directed more toward the state and away from God. To keep church and state separate is to keep Jesus, not our country, at the center of our worship. There is a place for patriotic displays, but our Lord told us not only to "Render to Caesar what is Caesar's," but also to give "to God what is God's."

Religious liberty and the separation of church and state also require that we not coerce others or pressure them into worshiping, praying, or acting in other ways as we do. Though some people claim it, neither God nor Bible reading nor prayers have been taken out of the public arena. Rather, the prohibition is on anything religious that is coerced or government sponsored. Baptists have always held that teaching and leading worship and prayer are the responsibilities of the church and the individual Christian—not the government. Therefore, as we build a distinctively Baptist church, let our worship be genuine, full, rich, and free.

Note

[1] Robert W. Pazmiño, *God Our Teacher: Theological Basics in Christian Education* (Grand Rapids MI: Baker Academics, 2001), 76.

Study Questions

1. "Worship" comes from an Anglo-Saxon word meaning "*worth*-ship." Read 1 Chronicles 29:10-18. How many reasons to worship God can you find in the passage?

_____

_____

_____

_____

2. In Isaiah 6:1-8, we find that God is worthy of worship because God is *holy*. How did Isaiah respond to his worship of God?

_____

_____

_____

_____

3. How does God change you when you worship Him?

_____

_____

_____

_____

4. What do you and your church do to experience each of these elements of worship?

• Music _____

• Scripture reading _____

• Silence_____

• Meditation_____

• Prayer_____

• Offering_____

• Invitation_____

• Preaching_____

Consider: How well do the ways your church members worship reflect Baptist distinctives? How could your worship become more distinctively Baptist?

Chapter 4

Building a Distinctively Baptist Church through Evangelism

Placing this chapter on evangelism after the one on worship does not suggest it is less important, but neither is it greater. Nor do we need to separate the two. Perhaps you already see and act on the close relationship between worship and evangelism. Obviously, there is more to evangelism than I can cover in this brief chapter. People have written hundreds of books on this vital topic and task. Even the best ones are incomplete. One goal of this chapter's short overview is to show how Baptist distinctives shape the way we share the gospel with others. Another goal is that reflection on evangelism will motivate us and our church's evangelistic attitudes and efforts.

What Is Evangelism?

To answer this question, we begin by examining one of the earliest acts of evangelism in the New Testament, found in Luke 2:8-14. It is also worship, demonstrating the relationship mentioned above. Notice that an angel appeared to the shepherds. After telling the shepherds not to be afraid, the angel explained why: there was "good news." After that announcement, a "multitude of heavenly hosts" joined the angel in praise and worship: "Glory to God in the highest" (NASB).

Notice that the word "angel" appears within the word "evangelism." This root suggests a lot about the believer's role in evangelism. "Angel" is actually the English version of the Greek *angelos*, which means "messenger." The subsequent root Greek word translated "good news" is *euangelon*. Again, the word for "messenger" appears at the center of the word. We believers are to be in the middle of evangelism. We might not be "angels" as typically understood, but we *are* God's messengers today.

What was the heavenly messenger's message? What was the good news that day? For them—and for us—a Savior, Jesus, had been born. What is *our* good news? Basically, it is the same news shared that day and for all time. However, within the call of the Great Commission in Matthew 28:18-20 is the instruction to baptize in the name of the Father, Son, and Holy Spirit. Therefore, we also understand that the message of salvation relates to *everything* God is.

First, *evangelism is telling and showing people how they can enter into covenant with God.* One aspect of the good news is that God calls people to covenant. The Hebrew word, *berith*, indicated a binding contract between two parties. These were often reciprocal with each side having particular responsibilities. This required a personal relationship. God invites Abraham to covenant in Genesis 12:1-3 and repeats the invitation in chapter 15. God's part of the agreement was to sustain and bless Abraham, and Abraham was to follow in faith. Though this particular covenant was between God and Abraham, a third person, Melchizedek, played a role. In Genesis 14:18-20, we read that Melchizedek was king of Salem (Jerusalem) and already a priest of God, whom Melchizedek knew as the Creator God and as *El Elyon*, or God Most High. Important is that Melchizedek recognized that the God with whom Abraham had a covenant was *El Elyon*. As a priest, Melchizedek blessed Abraham in that name. Thus, Abraham came to know God by a name and in a new way. Hebrews 5–6 compares the role of Jesus to that of Melchizedek (and Psalm 110:4 connects Melchizedek with the line of David, which includes Jesus). The significance is that, through Jesus, people can know God in a new way.

God's agreement continued through Abraham's descendants, the people of Israel. Through Moses and Jeremiah, the covenant was shaped so that God would be Israel's God and they would be God's people (Exod 6:7 and Jer 7:23). Through Moses, in Exodus 9:4-6, God called Israel to fulfill the covenant by being "a kingdom of priests and a holy nation" (NASB).

God's covenants are often said to reveal God's character in terms of His holiness. Certainly God is holy. The Mosaic Law repeatedly calls for Israel to be holy because God is holy. But, through covenant, God is also characterized by mercy and grace, concepts not unique to the New Testament.

There are frequent references in the Old Testament to *chesed*, which can be translated "steadfast love," "loving kindness," or "grace." Psalm 25:6,

Psalm 69:16, Jeremiah 31:3, and Isaiah 63:7 are passages in which *chesed* describes what God offers to His people. Jeremiah 9:24 speaks of *chesed* in terms of a characteristic of God: "but let him who boasts boast of this, that he understands and knows Me, that I am the LORD who exercises lovingkindness, justice and righteousness on earth; for I delight in these things" (NASB). Like the grace we understand from the New Testament, *chesed* in the Old Testament begins with God. It is not the result of what people are or do.

God's call to covenant was an act of grace and mercy. Abraham was not perfect. No references to qualities of Abraham and his character indicate that he "earned" God's offer of a personal relationship. Rather, it was freely given, and Abraham followed. Nor was Abraham perfect during the rest of his life. There were times when Abraham exhibited great trust in God. The offering of Isaac in Genesis is one example. However, there were also times when Abraham lacked faith and even honesty. In Genesis 12, Abraham encourages his wife Sarah to mislead Pharaoh about their relationship. In Genesis 16, Abraham demonstrates a lack of faith in God by fathering a son through the handmaid Hagar. But ultimately, Abraham trusted God and God sustained him.

Even the Mosaic Law refers to God's mercy. Of course, as already noted, it also stresses God's holiness and the expectation of holiness from Israel, the people of the covenant. Further, the sacrifices and other demands of the Mosaic Law stress the seriousness and costliness of covenant. It is offered freely, but there are demands. God is indeed a God of grace, but we must never forget the cost. Nevertheless, God deeply desires covenant with people today. That is the basis of evangelism and, indeed, good news.

Second, *evangelism is telling and showing people how they can accept the Son as Lord, Redeemer, and Savior.* Romans 3:23 is a clear reminder that, like Abraham, none of us is perfect. We are sinners. The result, according to Romans 6:23, is death. The same passage, however, also gives *very* good news: God offers eternal life through Jesus. Through His grace, God still calls us to relationship in covenant. God's grace cost the life of His Son, Jesus the Christ.

"Atonement" is a word that describes reparation for a wrong. It relates to a covenant relationship. As described above, a covenant brings two parties together in relationship. To break the covenant is to divide the two participants. Atonement is the process to heal this breach. In the Mosaic Law, one atoned through sacrifice. Hebrews 9:26 is one of many passages about the good news that *Jesus* is the sacrifice for our atonement.

Another New Testament word that describes this process is "redemption"—when something of little or no worth gains or regains value. It is like repairing something that has been broken. Jesus died to restore worth to and repair our broken relationship with God (Gal 3:13; 4:5). A "right" or "righteous" covenant relationship was one in which each party kept its terms of the agreement. Similarly, an Israelite was called "just" or "justified" if he lived according to God's law. Romans 3:24 connects redemption and justification in terms of our relationship with God; we are "justified as a gift by His grace through the redemption which is in Christ Jesus" (NASB). Ephesians 1:7 puts it more graphically: "In Him we have redemption through His blood, the forgiveness of our trespasses, according to the riches of His grace" (NASB).

Is there *anything* required of the individual? Certainly. When the Philippian jailer asked him what was required to be saved, Paul replied, "Believe in the Lord Jesus" (Acts 16:31, NASB). This relates to one's faith. We can define faith as having something upon which we center or focus our lives. The object of our faith is our ultimate and defining concern. In this sense, faith is universal. After all, *everyone* has *something* that gives their lives meaning. *Everyone* has *something* that is his or her most essential concern. Jesus explores this idea with the "rich young ruler" in Matthew 19:16-22, Mark 10:17-22, and Luke 18:18-23. Jesus challenged the man to reexamine the focus of his life, asking himself, "Where is my faith?" Sadly, it was in his wealth. A happier result happened when, in Luke 19:1-9, Zaccheus made a similar self-examination. Zaccheus's pledge (in v. 8) showed his faith. That is, he changed the object of his ultimate concern. In verse 9, Jesus celebrates that change by observing, "Today salvation has come to this house" (NASB).

That commitment and shift in focus is part of the significance of one's being "born again." Jesus offers this challenge to Nicodemus in John 3:3. Such drastic change in a person's life means a totally new orientation. It is not merely adherence to a narrow, culturally defined set of morals, behaviors, or prohibitions. Everything is changed. As Paul puts it in 2 Corinthians 5:1, "Therefore if anyone is in Christ, he is a new creature; the old things passed away; behold, new things have come" (NASB).

Can a person truly make that kind of change? No. It requires our willingness and commitment, but the actual change is beyond us. Another part of the good news is that God can and will change us. Jesus also told

Nicodemus that the power for rebirth is found only through one's trust in the death of God's "only begotten Son" (John 3:5-6, 14-21).

A commitment to Jesus also means a commitment to live in opposition to sin. Therefore, the first step a person takes toward Jesus is repentance. To repent means to "turn away." Jesus, as one person of the Trinity, is holy. As a person—God incarnate—Jesus lived a sinless life. Simply stated, one cannot embrace sin and Jesus at the same time. Salvation is not "fire insurance." It entails our commitment to covenant and to trust what God promises to bring to the relationship. God has committed; what is lacking is *our* commitment.

When Jesus redeems us, God restores our relationship and covenant with Him. We realize or receive atonement, and wonderful things happen. Jesus promises His presence with us now and forever. He assures us of eternal life. To bear witness of this work of Jesus is the sum of the Christian's role in evangelism.

Third, *evangelism is telling and showing people how the Holy Spirit can change them.* The Holy Spirit is *not* another God. God the Holy Spirit is one of the three persons of the Trinity. As is true with all other persons of God, the Holy Spirit has important roles to play in evangelism.

First, the Holy Spirit changes us by convicting us of our sin and our sinful nature. The Holy Spirit awakens us to our need for God. Jesus describes this role of the Holy Spirit in John 16:8: "And He, when He comes, will convict the world concerning sin and righteousness and judgment" (NASB).

Second, according to Jesus in John 3:6 and 8, the Holy Spirit changes us by being the agent by which we experience rebirth.

Third, the Holy Spirit changes us by sanctifying us. Sanctification is the process by which God the Holy Spirit makes us holy (something we are powerless to do ourselves). Paul connects the Holy Spirit to sanctification in Romans 15:16.

Fourth, the Holy Spirit changes us by entrusting certain gifts to us. Those spiritual gifts are given for us to use in God's service and to build up God's Kingdom and God's church. Paul addresses this issue in 1 Corinthians 12–14.

Fifth, the Holy Spirit changes us by giving power and courage that are beyond us. The Holy Spirit grants this courage and power so that Christians will be able to carry out God's will and use their gifts as intended. In Romans

15:18-19, Paul credits the power of the Holy Spirit for what he has been able to accomplish.

God requires many changes in the lives of sinful people. We cannot change ourselves. It seems hopeless, but there is hope. It is good news. In His grace, God will effect those changes if and when people are willing. But how can people know these things if no one tells them? Isaiah 52:7 and Romans 10:15 agree: "how beautiful are the feet" of those who tell others the good news.

How, then, are we to tell and show people about the gospel, the good news? There are two simple steps. Christians must do their jobs. We must also let God (Father, Son, and Holy Spirit) do God's work.

In Matthew 5:13-14, we find two images that summarize our work in evangelism: salt and light. We can apply these images to Christians in many ways. As light, Christians share the gospel by reflecting the Light that is our Lord, Jesus. As salt, we evangelize by living so that people become thirsty for Jesus, the Living Water.

Delos Miles once described the work of Christians in evangelism as having three dimensions: being, doing, and telling the gospel.[1] Matthew 4:23 shows how Jesus modeled those dimensions. Of course, Jesus *was* the gospel. Jesus *did* the gospel by healing people. Jesus *proclaimed* the gospel. Similar references to Jesus sharing the good news by word and deed fill the four Gospels of the New Testament. As we look at how we can fulfill these dimensions of evangelism, we must remember the importance of all three. No single one completes our task. Describing or designing any solid object requires the use of the three dimensions of height, width, and depth. Using only one results in almost nothing. Using two dimensions leaves the object flat. Likewise, if our outreach uses only one of these dimensions, we do little. Using two of them still leaves our efforts flat. For our evangelism to be solid, we must incorporate all three dimensions.

As did Jesus, we evangelize by *embodying* the gospel. Jesus is often spoken of as the Incarnation, or as God in the Flesh. However, Christians, as the church, are the body of Christ, or Jesus in the flesh today. This requires that our evangelism begin within us. Francis of Assisi is credited saying it this way: "While you are proclaiming peace with your lips, be careful to have it even more fully in your heart." Further, he advocated putting it into action: "Preach the gospel at all times and when necessary use words." Jesus' description of discipleship in Matthew 16:24 outlines the three steps toward embodying the gospel as Jesus did: self-denial, sacrificial service, and faithful following. The result is that we become the "fragrance of Christ" to the lost (2 Cor 2:15).

Like Jesus, we evangelize by *doing* the gospel. The good news is that God cares about physical as well as spiritual needs. The New Testament gives numerous examples of Jesus meeting both kinds of needs. Jesus often connected healing and feeding with proclamation of the good news. He even linked them as signs of His Kingdom's arrival. How can we do the gospel? In Matthew 25:31-40, Jesus answers that question. It is simple, though not always easy. We do the gospel by meeting the needs of people as we encounter them.

One request in the Lord's Prayer is twofold: God's kingdom come and God's will be done. When we do the gospel, God answers that request. By doing what Jesus did, we live as God's Kingdom. By doing the gospel, we do God's will, because it is God's will for all to be saved (2 Pet 3:9).

Following Jesus, we evangelize by *proclaiming* the gospel. Even this dimension requires more than we often realize. We usually think of telling people about Jesus' life, death, and resurrection and how they relate to people's lives, sin, and eternity. At that point, the good news is that God loves them and has made a way for everyone—despite sin—to spend eternity with Him. Judgment and accountability are also a part of the story. However, according to John 3:16-17, grace and love lie at the heart of the gospel.

People also need to hear from Christians more words of grace than words of judgment and condemnation. Jesus witnessed to this in John 8:3-11. His response to the situation had two parts: grace (non-condemnation) and accountability (the challenge to sin no more). Often, our temptation is to overlook one and focus on the other, but both are vital. For the woman to appreciate Jesus' gift of grace, she had to know the seriousness of her sin. Likewise, the more she grasped the wonder of grace, the more earnestly she would live as God intended.

Typically, we find a great challenge in finding the balance Jesus demonstrated. It seems that we do not hate sin enough and we do not love sinners enough. We hate the sins of others, of course, and those sins we are not tempted to commit. But we seem not to hate *our* sin enough. On the other hand, we love our kind of sinner adequately, but not those who differ from us. This may have been part of what Jesus taught in Matthew 7:1-2 and John 8:15. After all, how can lost people comprehend that the Holy God loves them despite their sin if they do not feel loved by us?

Notice that, in the New Testament, Jesus does not proclaim the gospel only in places of worship. He did worship and teach in the synagogues and in the temple. However, Jesus also preached the gospel wherever He went. Our call, then, is to proclaim the good news beyond the church sanctuary. Our evangelism should include words and deeds of witness in our homes, schools, and places of work. In other words, we are witnesses in our everyday lives.

We have a great responsibility to evangelize. However, more of the good news is that, in and through God's power, Christians can do what they are called to do. All else is God's work in evangelism.

Therein lay the great problems in evangelism. Christians can become so overwhelmed and threatened by the task before them that they freeze and do little or nothing. My advice is that we do our jobs. Remember first that, in evangelism, Jesus has already done the hard part. We are called to witness to what he did. Jesus suffered and died on the cross. Also keep in mind that God will always empower people to do what He calls them to do. Further, God promises His presence to those who seek to do His will.

Another problem is that many Christians seem to think they must do God's part in evangelism. My advice, again, is that we do our jobs. Our task is not to "win the lost"; the victory belongs to Jesus. Remember Jesus' dialogue with the "rich young ruler" in Matthew 19:16-22? Jesus shared with the man what he needed to do and left the decision up to him. The young man walked away, retaining his wealth and rejecting Jesus. Jesus did not run after him, but we can be sure Jesus' heart was breaking. (And later, Jesus still died on the cross for that man as well as for us.)

We *are* called to be witnesses and to speak with conviction. However, Christians are not called to argue the lost into heaven. Some may cite the statement of the master in Jesus' Parable of the Dinner (Luke 14:15-24). In verse 23, he commands a servant to go out to others and "compel them to come in" (NASB). *Anagkason* is the Greek word translated "compel." Some versions of the Bible also translate the word "make" or "constrain." That may sound as if our evangelistic task as Jesus' servants is to force people into salvation. However, *anagkason* relates more to urgency in reaching out to others. Also, as we all know, no person can be forced into salvation. Genuinely being born again requires one's being drawn and convicted by the Holy Sprit. Anyone trying to force or coerce another into a profession of faith will more likely produce either a hardened heart or a hypocrite.

Our call and task is to bear testimony, not to twist arms. The task of the Holy Spirit is to convict and convince. A pastor friend of mine often said the following when offering the invitation at the end of a worship service: "Anything I can talk you into, someone else can talk you out of. Listen to God. He is speaking to you. Do what the Holy Spirit is leading you to do."

Evangelism in the Lives of Believers and Churches

What role does evangelism play in the life of the individual Christian and of each church? First, *evangelism gives a twofold purpose.* One part is that we be witnesses. In Acts 1:8, Jesus tells His disciples that they will be witnesses. To witness simply means to testify regarding what one knows and has experienced. The first Christian witness spoke the simple—yet wonderful—phrase "Jesus is risen." What does our witness tell others about what we have seen and experienced? In other words, what kind of witnesses are we?

The second part is that we make disciples. We can describe the Great Commission of Matthew 28:18-20 by breaking it into parts: go, make disciples, baptize, and teach. However, it seems better to understand those parts as a whole or a system. What matters most is the synergistic relationship among the components. We also have Jesus' presence to encourage, guide, and empower us.

Second, *evangelism leads to growth.* This growth may not be in the most obvious area. Our contemporary culture places great emphasis on numeric growth. Where and when numerical growth matters, it relates to the increase of God's Kingdom. Although gospel outreach may lead to numeric growth for a church, this should not be the motive. Our reason for evangelism should be that our Lord has called and commanded us to do it. Through His grace, Jesus makes us partners in redeeming a hurting world. That ought to be enough.

When churches and individual Christians evangelize, they can count on other kinds of growth. Sharing the gospel is spiritual exercise. It strengthens our faith and helps us grow. A muscle used in physical exercise increases in tone and in strength. The same occurs with evangelism. A church focused on evangelism grows stronger. It becomes more aware of its witness to the community. Its members are more aware of what brings them together in a common purpose than what differs among them. A Christian who centers his or her life on evangelism also becomes spiritually stronger. When we concentrate on Jesus' call and presence, our evangelism becomes more sensitive to and aware of Him. As a result, we are less susceptible—though never immune—to temptations. Because of this, we can grow to "live in a manner worthy" of our role as the redeemed (1 Thess 2:12).

Finally, when we witness, our humility increases. Paul's brief summary of the gospel message in Ephesians 2:8-9 is a call to avoid arrogance. We cannot share the gospel without remembering that only God's grace makes it possible.

Third, *evangelism leads to encouragement.* The world is a tough place full of bad news. All of us, the saved and the lost, need encouragement. We all need good news. The unsaved need the encouragement of knowing God's love and the hope found in salvation.

Have you ever thought of how evangelism affects even those who are saved? Nowhere in the Bible are we called to witness only to the unsaved. No matter how long we have been saved, we find encouragement in evangelism. It happens when we hear of God's work in the lives of other Christians. Even when we share the witness, we are reminding ourselves of the wonder of God's grace, mercy, and power. Joshua 4:7 and 1 Samuel 7:12 relate accounts of Israel establishing memorials to miraculous works of God. They helped the people recall God's delivering His people. Each moment of evangelism reminds us of the same message. That is good news and a wonderful source of encouragement in difficult times.

For each Christian and church, then, evangelism must be more than a program. It should be holistic. Outreach must include everything that each person and church is and does. Some would select being either a verbal or a lifestyle witness. To follow the example of Jesus, we must be both. Only then can we fulfill our purpose and experience the growth and encouragement found in evangelism.

Baptist Distinctives and Evangelism

The Authority of Scripture

Evangelism, as with everything we do as Christians and as churches, should be carried out under the leadership of the Holy Spirit. One way we discern that leadership is by looking to the Bible. The authority of Scripture requires that evangelism among Baptists be biblically based. This shapes the message, motivation, and methods of a Baptist church's evangelistic efforts.

Baptists must be certain that the message it shares in evangelism is consistent with Scripture. This may seem obvious. However, we easily overlook a significant element. The fullness of evangelism means sharing how one can accept the free gift of God. Jesus paid the price of our sin. We cannot earn and can never deserve God's grace and mercy. However, Jesus did teach that discipleship requires something of us (Luke 14:26-35). To leave that out of the gospel is to preach what some call "cheap grace." Committing and submitting one's life to the Lordship of Jesus requires self-denial and a life of sacrificial service (Matt 16:24). Salvation is not the result of works. It comes through faith. Ephesians 2:8-9 and Romans 1:17 are only two of the many passages that emphasize this. However, James 2:14-26 reminds us that it is essential, perhaps even inevitable, for Christ-like living to result from genuine faith.

Baptists must also be sure that their motives in evangelism are pure and based on biblical principles and teachings. First Corinthians 10:31 and 2 Corinthians 4:6 are clear that the desire to glorify God should motivate evangelism. When our longing to glorify God drives evangelism, no room remains for egocentricity and self-aggrandizement. As in the true worship of the elders in Revelation 4, all the glory belongs to Jesus, the Lamb.

When the praise of God motivates our evangelism, we remember our goal: to make disciples. That means we reach out to people so that they become disciples of *Jesus*. They are not to be *our* disciples. Our aim and desire is that they grow to resemble Jesus, not us.

Of course, when we hold the Bible as authoritative, the Bible shapes the methods of our outreach. This includes a church and its members being living witnesses. Our lives—separately and together—must reflect God's holiness. We must also live consistently the love of God found in Jesus. To do otherwise is to contradict the gospel we proclaim. Consider the tragic irony of Christians of the eighteenth and nineteenth centuries complying with and participating in the evil of the slave trade. We must maintain a keen sensitivity so that we do not fall prey to wrongs that would hinder our gospel witness.

There are countless examples of how the Bible should influence the ways we evangelize. Some suggest how we should *not* do evangelism. Others reveal ways we *should* witness. For the sake of illustration, let us look at one instance of each.

Sometimes we are tempted to say we will do *anything* to reach out to the lost. That sentiment is admirable. However, we must remember that our methods sometimes work counter to our goals. For example, what we say in evangelism must be the truth. To say otherwise is to break the ninth commandment. One practical application is that we need not elaborate our testimony to render it more dramatic. Further, Ephesians 4:15 requires that we always speak words of witness in and with love. A harsh, hateful, angry word of witness—even if it is true—belies the love, grace, and mercy with which God reaches out to sinful humanity. First Corinthians 13 elaborates on the same principle.

A positive example of the Bible shedding light on our methods of evangelism is found in Acts 17:22-34. That passage tells of Paul's speech before the council of philosophers on Mars Hill in Athens. Though surrounded by altars and idols to false gods, Paul did not condemn the people. Rather, he observed how religious the Athenians were. They even had an altar to an unknown god! Paul seized that opportunity to tell them about God, who was unknown to them. In his speech, Paul used some words and concepts of Greek philosophies to communicate the gospel. That is an important lesson for evangelism. We should shape our witness in words and terms that are understandable to the culture of the hearers.

Recognizing the authority of Scripture requires that we evangelize. Importantly, it requires that we take care in considering the what, why, and how of our outreach.

The Priesthood of All Believers

The priesthood of all believers addresses the "who" of evangelism. Evangelism is critical to the priestly function. It is a task for every member of the priesthood and not only for the clergy or the "professionals." In 2 Corinthians 5:17-20, Paul writes that as "new creatures," those reconciled to God are called to the "ministry of reconciliation." The priesthood does not save a person. However, through salvation one enters the priesthood.

This is not to deny that the Bible teaches that, for some, evangelism is a special calling. Consider, for example, Ephesians 4:11. However, if *all* Jesus' disciples are to obey the Great Commission, all believers are to do evangelism. We are, indeed, sinners, but God still wants to use us to reach out to others. In Spanish, the word for "sinner" is *pecador*. *Pescador* is the Spanish word for "fisherman." Only one letter makes the difference between the two words. Just as Jesus called His first disciples, God uses each saved sinner (*pecador*) to be a "fisherman" (*pescador*) for souls through evangelism (Matt 4:19 and Mark 1:17).

The priesthood of all believers requires each Christian to be a living witness. This means living pure and holy lives. It also means each priest should be a living example of God's grace, love, and mercy. It has often been said Christians are the only Bible some people will ever read.

Perhaps a better way to put it is that each Christian is the only Jesus some people will ever see. Many years ago, a layman introduced himself to me this way: "I am a disciple of Jesus cleverly disguised as a welder." What a wonderful way to see one's self and one's role in evangelism! That is why God wants to change and transform us—so that we are changed to be more like Jesus.

How then should believers function as the priesthood? First, we accept our responsibilities as priests. That means sharing with others as Jesus did. It means putting aside personal preferences to follow our call. It means having pure motives. It means being more redemptive and less judgmental.

For the priesthood of all believers, evangelism is not a rite of passage. It is a call and a privilege of the highest order. The call is to incarnational ministry and evangelism. Just as with salvation, God accepts each believer/priest as he or she is. Then, though His power, God nurtures and changes us as His disciples. As Jesus puts it in Matthew 9:37-38, "the harvest is plentiful," and "beseech the Lord of the harvest to send out workers into His harvest" (NASB). As God's royal priesthood, we should pray that we each see God, hear God's call, and respond as Isaiah does in Isaiah 6:1-8: "Here am I. Send me!"

The Autonomy of the Local Church

Since the autonomy of the local church results from the priesthood of all believers, the previous section applies to this one. There are further observations, however.

Since each church is autonomous, each is free to evangelize as it sees fit. Of course, it could be argued that this responsibility should begin within the church and at its doorstep. Then it should radiate outward. That sounds like Jesus' command to His disciples (in Acts 1:8) to be witnesses to Jerusalem, Judea, Samaria, and, ultimately, the entire earth. Further, the local church knows best how to shape its fellowship into a force for evangelism.

As we have seen, evangelism is an enormous job. To think in terms of witnessing to the whole world boggles the mind! That is why each church must do its share of the task—whatever that means for a specific group of believers. We have also noted that evangelism requires creative approaches that speak to diverse situations and cultures. That is why each church must reach out to the culture and community it knows best and in which it exists. However, that should not be the end of a church's evangelistic efforts. It is only the beginning.

Some have described a church as being like a bed of coals. If a burning ember is separated from the others, it soon burns out. Together, however, the coals remain hotter longer. The fellowship of believers in the church serves a similar purpose. This is especially true with evangelism. A church should be a place where the fires of evangelism among its members burn hotter, brighter, and longer.

A church can fan these fires in many ways. At the risk of mixing metaphors, we will examine some of the ways using the image of Christians being sowers of the gospel's seeds.

First, each church has the responsibility to create sowers. Of course, Jesus actually creates the believer. The point is that the church is responsible to witness so that people have the opportunity to respond to the gospel and accept Jesus as Lord. Then, each church must call the sowers. Not every new Christian (not even every "old" Christian) is aware of his or her individual responsibilities as a witness. The church should nurture that awareness. Once believers are aware of their evangelistic call, they need training. Even the best-intentioned efforts can be misguided. Findley B. Edge once described the danger: "defective evangelism contributes to unregenerate church membership."[2] Thus, for evangelism to be more effective, the church must train and equip the sowers. Training them is the first step. Additionally, the church must budget its resources to provide the sowers the tools they need to do their job. The church should also send the sowers. That is part of the meaning of Romans 10:15. By sending each other out as witnesses, church members are accountable for and to each other. Similarly, the church is to encourage the sowers. Due to personal matters as well as barriers in our evangelistic efforts, we can become discouraged. We need the support of others. If every member of a church urges all the others in this task, every person receives confidence. The joint witness is often more powerful than that of the lone witness. A church working together to advance the gospel bears testimony to diverse people loving and accepting each other despite their differences.

We often refer to evangelism as "outreach." Outreach means that evangelism is more than simply getting people to church on Sunday. It means *being* the church in the world *every day*. That is possible only if each church acts on its own and as God leads it. However, each Baptist church must remember the other side of autonomy: cooperation. No church needs to do evangelism alone. Rather, it is free to join with other churches and Christians in outreach efforts. This is often done in cooperation with other Baptist churches. Sometimes it is within the context of an association or convention of Baptist churches. Also, many Baptist churches work with churches of other denominations in evangelistic crusades to reach out to their community. Such cooperation offers its own kind of witness, testimony, and encouragement.

Autonomy leaves each church free to act creatively and with integrity, using the individual and corporate gifts God has entrusted to it. No one can coerce a church into one form or method of evangelism. Rather, each body of Christ has the right (and responsibility) to design its own ministry of evangelism—to the glory of the Lord.

The Ordinances of Baptism and the Lord's Supper

Both baptism and the Lord's Supper are evangelistic events in at least two ways. First, through acting out the drama of redemption, they tell the good news. Baptism tells that Jesus died for us, was buried, and rose from the dead to give us the promise of eternal life. Baptism also tells the story that the one being baptized, in committing his or her life to the Lordship of Jesus, has died to the old life of sin and rises to a new, eternal life with Him. The simple, yet profound story of the Lord's Supper tells of Jesus' sacrifice given to cleanse us of our sins.

However, the ordinances are also opportunities for Christians to be witnesses and tell the story themselves. Obviously, in baptism, the candidate testifies to what she or he has experienced. Further, both ordinances afford occasion to explain their meaning as the church observes them. They also create opportunities for non-Christians to ask their Christian friends the meaning of these important and meaningful rituals.

Further, through their observation, both are occasions for all who participate to reflect and be encouraged. They can find inspiration for further testimony and fellowship. By reflecting on their own conversions, they may rediscover the joy of their salvation as the psalmist seeks in Psalm 51:12.

The ordinances are not simply the results of evangelism. They offer tremendous potential for a distinctively Baptist church to *do* evangelism. Each church must explore ways it can observe these ordinances to stress their importance and message and to employ them more effectively in evangelism.

Religious Liberty and the Separation of Church and State

The ways religious liberty and the separation of church and state can shape evangelism in a Baptist church are summarized in two words: clarification and freedom.

This vital concept helps us clarify our agenda for evangelism. History provides many examples of how, when church and state intermingle, the point of evangelism usually gets lost and allegiances get confused. It becomes almost impossible to sort out what is "Caesar's" and what is God's. The point of evangelism is to lead others to become more like Jesus, not to be more patriotic.

The separation of church and state also clarifies the nature of our evangelistic goals. As early English Baptists John Smyth and Thomas Helwys observed, the aims and authority of civil government are temporal and secular. On the contrary, the goals of evangelism relate to eternity and the sacred, underscoring the vital importance and urgency of evangelism.

Keeping church and state separate clarifies the need to submit to what Jesus commands in Matthew 7:12 and Luke 6:31. Evangelism requires a certain zeal and boldness. However, part of what our Lord taught us in the "Golden Rule" was to respect rights of others. Non-Christians are entitled to the same freedoms each Christian has under law. Our evangelistic efforts must always respect the rights and freedoms of others.

There are many ways religious liberty and the separation of church and state free churches and Christians to do the work of evangelism. First, because of this vital concept, evangelism *can* happen. That is, under this wonderful freedom there is no sword pointed at our throats. There are no threats of torture or imprisonment if we share about or receive Jesus. Commitment of the heart can happen only when people are *free* to accept *or* reject the gospel as their hearts dictate. Our evangelism, therefore, is all the more vital. Everyone should have the opportunity to accept or reject God.

Separation of church and state means Baptists and Baptist churches are free from governmental interference that inhibits evangelism. Of course, this is balanced with the government's responsibility to protect the rights and freedoms of others. Civil authorities must be impartial in what they allow and permit. Churches need to keep this in mind when planning and performing their outreach. A church cannot expect to be allowed access and privileges forbidden to other religious groups.

Churches established by a state receive financial support through tax revenues. They also have special access to government services and assistance not permitted to others. The freedom found in the separation of church and state frees Baptist churches from governmental support of any kind. Our efforts on God's behalf are genuinely our own. We support our witness through our offerings—to God—of time, talent, and money. The significance goes beyond that of our "owning" our evangelism. It also means our work and witness cannot be constrained. In its crucial work of evangelism, a Baptist church should always remember its heritage. That includes the sacrifices and deaths of many forebears who called for religious liberty and church/state separation. A Baptist church must never, intentionally or not, put evangelism or its heritage up for sale.

Considered together, Baptist distinctives challenge each church to fulfill its evangelistic call and task. They give us four reasons why Baptist churches should never neglect evangelism: The cost is too dear. The mandate is too clear. The need is too great. The resources are too numerous.

Notes

[1] Delos Miles, *Introduction to Evangelism* (Nashville: Broadman Press, 1983), 49.

[2] Findley B. Edge, *A Quest for Vitality in Religion*, rev. edition (Macon GA: Smyth & Helwys, 1994), 157.

Study Questions

1. Fill in the blanks. The bad news is that _____

   (Romans 3:23). The bad news is that _____

   (Romans 6:23a). The good news is that _____

   (Romans 6:23b). The good news is that _____

   (John 3:16).
2. Fill in the blanks of these statements about evangelism from chapter 4. The term "evangelism" comes from a Greek word that means

   _____ _____.

Evangelism rises from God's desire to _____ Himself to creation.

Evangelism is _____ and _____ people how they can enter into _____ with God.

Evangelism is _____ and _____ people how they can _____ the Son as _____, _____, and _____.

Evangelism is _____ and _____ people how they can be _____ by the _____ _____.

Like Jesus, we can evangelize by _____, _____, and _____ the gospel.

Evangelism gives us _____, leads to _____ of God's Kingdom, and _____ Christians.

3. How are you and your church doing the various aspects of evangelism?

_____

_____

_____

_____

4. What motivates you and your church to do evangelism?

_____

_____

_____

_____

5. How can each Baptist distinctive help you and your church build a more
   effective evangelism ministry?

_____

_____

_____

_____

Building a Distinctively Baptist Church through Missions

Every day we hear about needs in our world: exploding world population, natural disasters, war, poverty. Consider the incredible advances in transportation and commerce and the fact that our local and world cultures are becoming more and more diverse. We read, see, and hear about political and religious hostility—with deadly results. People crave intimacy yet are becoming more isolated from each other.

Missions dares the church to meet these many, diverse needs. What a tremendous challenge! What an opportunity!

It may be difficult to believe that missions has not always been at the heart of Baptist life. As we saw in the first chapter, William Carey instigated a move toward missions. Interest in missions grew through Luther Rice and the Judsons, eventually leading to the establishment of the Triennial Convention. When Baptists of the South separated from the Triennial Convention, their urgency for missions did not diminish. On Friday, May 9, 1845, the first Southern Baptist Convention passed a resolution stating that "for the maintenance of those scriptural principles . . . it is proper that this Convention at once proceed to organize a Society for the propagation of the Gospel."[1]

Christian missions is closely linked to evangelism. Actually, when the two are done well, they are inseparable. Therefore, what we learned about evangelism in the previous chapter is equally true in this one. It is essential that evangelism—in its fullest sense—permeates all we do in missions. In the previous chapter, we saw how a church functions as a living witness. That is exactly what missions is—living the gospel.

The aim of this chapter is to explore how Baptist heritage can shape and form a church with the same sense of urgency. This is not an extensive treatment of theology or strategies of missions. Rather, as an overview, I will try to answer the why, what, where, how, and who questions of missions work. Then I will explore the application and influence of Baptist distinctives on a church's work in and through missions.

Why Should We Do Missions?

Like evangelism, missions rises from the very nature of God, especially His grace and all-inclusive love. God seeks a relationship with His Creation. Our loving God is also sovereign, the ruler of the universe. Toward those ends, God has always worked to reveal Himself to the world.

How has God chosen to reveal Himself? Nature shows us his majestic beauty. More clearly and directly, God reveals Himself through the Bible. The Bible tells us that Jesus, God the Son, is the ultimate revelation of God. Through Isaiah 7:1 and Matthew 1:23, we learn that, in fact, Jesus *is* Immanuel or "God with us."

Yet God reveals Himself to the world in another way: through His people. That means you and me. Since God is our Sovereign Lord, we do as He orders. Both Old and New Testaments record God's calling of His people to show the world about Him. We will explore several examples.

In Genesis 12:1, God calls Abram (later named Abraham), "Go forth from your country . . . To the land which I will show you." Then, in 12:3, God gives Abraham the ultimate purpose: "in you all the families of the earth will be blessed" (NASB). The obvious call was for Abraham to follow in faith. It required him to leave the familiarity of his comfort zone and go to an unknown place. The basis for God's aim in calling Abraham—to bless all humanity—was His steadfast love for humanity. God repeats this basis in His covenant statement to Abraham's son, Isaac, in Genesis 26:4.

Another, well-known instance of God's call to missions involves Moses. We find the story in Exodus 3–4. Moses' adult life was not as glamorous as what he had experienced growing up in Pharaoh's court in Egypt. Moses was a fugitive working as a shepherd for his father-in-law. He had a shady past, but at least he had a job. He was safe. Considering the alternatives, Moses was doing well.

God, however, had other plans for Moses. The people of Israel were suffering in Egypt. God wanted to meet their needs and free them from their misery. We often overlook God's reason for freeing them: so that they could serve God and become a blessing to the nations as God had promised. Moses offered a series of excuses not to go, including his lack of resources and abilities. God responded to each excuse and promised to provide what Moses needed. Some resources were of a material nature, such as his staff. Others, such as the miracles and signs God pledged, were supernatural. One, Aaron, was human. The greatest resource of all, however, was God's presence (Exod 3:12).

What does the example of Moses teach us? God sometimes calls people to service through unusual circumstances. God's call to missions often interrupts our complacency and, perhaps, our safety. God calls people regardless of their past. God still calls to meet needs of people. He wants them free to serve Him. Further, God always provides the resources people need to fulfill their mission. Finally, God always promises His presence.

Long after Moses, Solomon prayed at the dedication of the temple in Jerusalem. That prayer, recorded in 1 Kings 8, shows the king's grasp of the missions purpose of Israel in general and the ultimate purpose of the temple itself "that all the peoples of the earth may know Your name, to fear You, as do Your people Israel, and that they may know that this house which I have built is called by Your name" (1 Kgs 8:43, NASB).

Through the prophet Isaiah, God reaffirmed the missions purpose of His people (Isa 49:6). In Jeremiah 1:5, God describes Jeremiah's mission as global. God commissioned Jonah to preach to Nineveh, home of Israel's great enemies. In Jonah 4:11, God chides the reluctant prophet by explaining His concern for Nineveh. Later, Babylon conquered Judah. Judah's leader was in exile in Babylon. There, God still used Daniel and Ezekiel to be His witnesses and to meet people's needs.

We find missions implications in many of the psalms. Psalm 60:7-8 includes both tribes of Israel and non-Israelites as God's possessions. Psalm 22:28 speaks of God's rule as extending beyond Israel. Psalm 66 includes calls for "all the earth" to praise God (vv. 1 and 4) and for people to spread that praise abroad (v. 8).

Any discussion of missions foundations in the New Testament must begin with Jesus. In their stories of Jesus' birth, both Matthew and Luke reveal the purpose for which Jesus was born. Angels in Matthew 1:21 and Luke 2:11 speak of Him as Savior. Of course, Jesus Himself describes this purpose of God in John 3:16. He accepts that impending role in John 12:27.

In addition to His task of eternal importance, there were other aspects of Jesus' mission. In Luke 4:43, He says, "I must preach the kingdom of God to the other cities also, for I was sent for this purpose" (NASB). Think about the many miracles Jesus did. Which ones come to mind? Giving sight to the blind? Cleansing the lepers? Making the lame able to walk? Feeding the multitudes? Casting out demons? Turning water into wine? Raising the dead? Beyond their supernatural nature, what do these miracles share? They all show that Jesus came to meet people's needs. In Matthew 20:28, Jesus clearly includes both His sacrifice and His service in a brief description of His mission.

The story of Jesus' washing His disciples' feet (in John 13:3-17) illustrates that Jesus' mission on earth was service. Important for us to remember is that, in verse 15 and 17, Jesus commands His disciples to follow His example of servanthood.

Missions-minded Baptists are familiar with Matthew 28:18-20, the "Great Commission." However, we easily overlook that it follows the disciples' worship of Jesus (Matt 28:17). Their worship, Jesus' claiming authority, and His command to go remind us of Isaiah's experience (Isa 6:1-9). John 20:21 records Jesus' telling His disciples something that reflects the service aspect of the Great Commission: "as the father has sent me, I also send you" (NASB). Just as Jesus' mission embodied the love, grace, and mercy of God, our lives are to reflect that of Jesus, our Servant-Lord.

The book of Acts begins with its own version of the Great Commission. In 1:4-8, Jesus ties the work of the disciples to the Holy Spirit. In the Matthew account, Jesus promises His presence. In Acts, Jesus explains that Presence. He would be with them through the Holy Spirit. In fact, we need to note that Jesus did not tell the disciples to go out immediately. He told them to await the coming of the Spirit. The disciples, as we do today, would need the Holy Spirit for strength and direction.

The remainder of Acts shows the fulfillment of Acts 1:4-8. The scope of the book begins, literally, in Jerusalem. It spreads from there and ends with Paul in Rome, partially fulfilling Acts 1:8: "you shall be My witnesses both in Jerusalem, and in all Judea and Samaria, and even to the remotest part of the earth" (NASB).

Acts also shows the work of the Holy Spirit in the mission of Christians. First, Acts 2 tells the story of the coming of the Holy Spirit at Pentecost. Many were saved as a result. We could fairly call this the beginning of Christian missions. Certainly, most of those new Christians went home after a time. We can safely assume that the eyewitnesses to such an event testified and did missions on their way and during the rest of their lives.

Further, throughout Acts, one can find references to Christians being led by the Holy Spirit. In Acts 8:29, the Holy Spirit directs Philip to speak to the

Ethiopian eunuch. The Holy Spirit similarly brought together Peter and Cornelius (Acts 1:19-20). Acts 13:1-3 records the Holy Spirit as the source of the Antioch church's missionary vision. Following the Spirit, the church sent Paul (or Saul, as he was known at that time) and Barnabas on a missionary journey.

Acts 16:6 and 20:22 relate examples of the Holy Spirit's guiding the direction of Christian missions. In the latter instance, Paul was "bound by the Spirit" to go to Jerusalem. He knew the mission was dangerous. Paul would need the Spirit's comfort and power to complete his call.

The entire Bible has much to say about why Christians should be involved in missions. Our Sovereign God, the Creator, came as His Son. Through all three Persons of the Trinity—Father, Son, and Holy Spirit—God calls each of us to salvation and missions service.

As Lord and Guide of our lives, He is also Lord and Guide of our missions work. The many demands for this work require a level of effort and discernment that is beyond human ability. Even if we accept that, as Christians, we are to be involved in missions, we still require God's presence to guide us as we consider the following questions regarding that work.

What Is Missions?

The Bible shows that missions has to do with God's self-revelation to the world. This means missions has many interrelated dimensions.

First, and most simply, *missions is following God.* Jesus puts it that way in Matthew 16:24. Our discipleship is an everyday matter. By following God, we do what Jesus did. We become servants. We sacrifice. We do what we can to meet people's needs. These needs may be spiritual or physical—perhaps both. Whatever the case, our lives for Jesus are to be lives of service.

Second, *missions is going for God.* Going implies starting where we are. However, it requires shaking off complacency. It usually means leaving the familiarity and safety of our comfort zones.

Third, *missions is making disciples for God.* This aspect of missions belongs in the middle of the list. It is closely (and equally) related to the preceding two aspects and the following two aspects. Making disciples, like being a disciple, is a never-ending process. A business term that describes the process well is "continuous quality improvement." Since Jesus made disciples, so should we. Making disciples demands that we look outside ourselves. Indeed, we become better disciples of Jesus as we lead others to do the same.

Making disciples starts with the work of evangelism. The beginning of a new Christian's discipleship is following Jesus in baptism. Making disciples involves teaching others obedience to their Lord.

Fourth, *missions is baptizing for God.* In summary, evangelism—as usually understood—is at the heart of this aspect. Missions efforts must include telling others the gospel and encouraging them to have and profess faith in Jesus Christ. One cannot be a disciple of Jesus without first having accepted Jesus as Lord. Then, that walk continues through confessing Jesus as Lord (Matt 10:32). Baptism is an act of confession. We help others to be disciples by presenting an opportunity for this act of obedience and holding them accountable.

Fifth, *missions is teaching for God.* The Great Commission reminds us that our missions efforts must include teaching disciples. The two primary facets of missions teaching are obedience and commands. The term "disciple" demands obedience. In John 10:27, Jesus says, "My sheep hear My voice, and I know them, and they follow Me" (NASB). What are Jesus' "sheep" (His disciples) to follow? The commands He gave them. As is often said of the Ten Commandments, these are *commands*, not *suggestions*.

The Great Commission also requires totality in our teaching. Jesus said we are to teach *all* He commanded. Jesus gave His disciples many commandments about various aspects of life and relationships. Two of them are what Jesus called the greatest commandment and the second, which He said was like the first: to love God (Deut 6:5) and to love one's neighbor (Lev 19:18). Just those two have almost infinite implications. Our teaching must cover as much of life as possible. That leaves us a lot to teach.

Beyond all others, the commands we teach should be those God gave. This indicates that the aim of missions is God-ward. Christian missions should not involve reculturation or enculturation, but relationship. The gospel is non-cultural in the human sense. That is, no culture, nation, state, or community is inherently Christian. These are human institutions, and, as a result, they "[sin] and fall short of the glory of God" as do individuals. As is true with evangelism, the purpose of missions is to make disciples *of Jesus,* not disciples of us or of our culture. The focus of missions is not to grow any earthly kingdom or culture, but to further *God's* Kingdom.

Where Can We Do Missions?

Once upon a time, Christians did not assume that they were to do missions anywhere and everywhere. The earliest Christians understood the global call of missions. That sense was somewhat lost during the Protestant Reformation. To end the Reformation's violence, Lutherans and Catholics developed an agreement called the Peace of Augsburg in 1555. The treaty stated that the religious perspective of the ruler of a given area determined the religion of that region. Of course, this protected Lutherans and Catholics, but not Anabaptists and other non-Lutherans/Catholics. This was part of the reason for the persecution Anabaptists endured as noted in chapter 1. Anabaptists and other dissenters who followed resisted those restrictions. They suffered as a result.

Momentum for missions changed in the late eighteenth century due to the influence of the Anabaptist Moravians. Soon, one could find Moravians doing missions work not only in Europe, but also in Greenland, the Caribbean, North America, Africa, and the Pacific. During the same time, William Carey (1761–1834) began the Baptist missions movement. As we have seen, in 1793, Carey's vision for missions took him from the church he pastored and his cobbler shop in England to India.

It is interesting that Carey did not use the term "foreign." Rather, he thought of missions in one direction: outward. Nevertheless, it remains helpful to see how missions is currently organized. This "outward" approach imitates the pattern of Acts 1:8, helps us understand the potential breadth of missions, and aids our appreciation of the common themes and tasks among missions strategies.

At its first meeting, the Southern Baptist Convention certainly looked at missions as an outward thrust. On Monday, May 12, 1845, that group passed a resolution establishing national or "domestic" and foreign missions agencies. The resolution also called for a missions presence in New Orleans (already a port city of national and international importance) and missions efforts to Native Americans ("Aborigines of America," it named them).[2]

After the local church, the first unit Baptists started was the association. This local body of churches originally had the purpose of providing mutual support among its member churches. Associations also have become the means by which churches unite in local missions outreach. Pooling their resources, the churches of a local association often can do more to discover and meet local needs than they could separately. The same can be said for state and international missions.

A distinctively Baptist church has a comprehensive vision. A missions vision that overlooks any one of the four geographical dimensions of missions—local, state, national, and international—is incomplete. This is especially true in our shrinking world.

Many Baptist churches, associations, and state and national conventions are finding that they are increasingly able to do international missions work without leaving home. Shifting immigration patterns are bringing the world to their doorsteps. Baptists and their churches are increasingly aware of the challenge of the Mosaic Law to care for "strangers" in their midst (Exod 22:21; Lev 19:34; Deut 10:19). They are welcoming those from other, often very different cultures. They are finding that ethnic missions without bias or exclusion is easier said than done. Nevertheless, they are trying. The result is that, in their respective contexts, local churches and associations are realizing the rich fabric of the Christian experience beyond what they had previously known. This is also the potential for those who venture into foreign, or international, missions. Means of communication and transportation have developed in such a way that awareness of needs overseas is much more possible than it once was. Likewise, it is also less difficult for people to journey to places overseas for the sake of missions.

Through the expanding, concentric circles of missions, Baptist churches can find ways to involve members in the missions strategies mentioned below. This increase in missions responsibility brings growing opportunities. However, the resources at our disposal have multiplied and improved. The same technological advances that have made our world a "global village" also offer tools by which to serve that village's needs.

How Can We Do Missions?

First, find a need. Next, find the resource to meet it. Finally, apply the resources to the need. It is that simple. Of course, we all usually need more direction than that. Nevertheless, what follows reflects application of this simple process. Notice something vital: all these methods and strategies relate to servanthood. As you and your church follow God's leadership into, through, and to missions, you will likely find other methods and strategies.

We do missions by understanding situations, tasks, and needs. This takes time and effort, but it is important. It is a matter of stewardship. God has provided us with many means by which to accomplish our missions tasks. As with all gifts entrusted to us by God, we are responsible for their wise and appropriate use. The roots of people's needs are not always apparent. Nor is the best way to meet them. By investing the time and effort to understand a particular situation, we can better grasp the most efficient and effective ways to serve through our time, talents, and finances.

We do missions by being relevant to the lives and needs of people. Of utmost importance is that we take time to relate to and/or identify with the people whom we seek to serve. That is one way to improve our grasp of the nature of their needs. Further, our service and our lives must connect with others in ways they understand, comprehend, and require. For example, in Matthew 25:31-36, Jesus does not say, "I was hungry and you gave me something to wear, I was thirsty and you visited me." The principle is not that the righteous had done just *anything*. Rather, what they did was relevant to the need.

We do missions by respecting (not merely tolerating) cultures. In and through our missions efforts, we likely will encounter cultures different from ours. Surely, we want people to respect our traditions. Obedience to the command of Jesus, then, requires that we respect the traditions of others. Moreover, missions service demands that we have the minds of servants. We are in that missions situation to serve the people and not be served. In 1 Corinthians 9:19-23, Paul expresses this principle well in his speech on Mars Hill (as noted in the previous chapter). When serving others, as Paul exemplified, we should respect their terms, vocabulary, gestures, dress.

The difficult task for most of us is to separate the core of the gospel from our background and traditions. However, this task is as vital as it is difficult. It is often complex and takes a lot of work. It does not mean "anything goes." There are aspects of every human culture that, under the light of Scripture, are counter to God's will. Rather, missions must be done in ways that both genuinely reflect the gospel and respect the traditions of those being served.

We do missions by showing God's love. Missions is not our effort to earn God's love. God loves us, pure and simple. We may not always be clear on the specific ways to serve others. Our attempts to understand the people and the need may fail us. We need not let confusion keep us from our task. If we know nothing else to do, we are to love. Indeed, we are to let God love others through us.

We do missions by praying. Our missions efforts will be in vain if they are devoid of prayer. Through prayer, we connect with God to find the awareness, insight, strength, love, grace, resources, patience, and other qualities necessary for the task. Through confession in prayer, we find forgiveness for times of failure (1 John 1:9). The "Lord's Prayer" of Matthew 6:9-13 is actually a great prayer for missions. In it we commit to obedience so that the Kingdom of God comes as God works in us and through us. Further, we ask only for "daily bread," not for luxury. This implies that one asks of God only that which is necessary to do Kingdom work. Our prayers should not only be for ourselves. They should also be prayers of intercession for all Christians. We should pray that we would all be on mission for our Lord and find His direction and resources to serve others in His Name.

Who Can Do Missions?—Missions in the Lives of Believers and a Church

God has chosen to invite His people to join Him in reaching out to a hurting world. It is an act of love and grace to us and through us. God's call to missions will influence the way we prioritize and shape our lives as Baptist churches and individuals. It will determine how we organize and we spend the time, energies, and other gifts God has entrusted to us.

Some have said that doing missions is God turning a church inside out. When we do that to our pockets, we see what they really contain. Similarly, career Baptist missionary and missiologist William O'Brien calls missions "the DNA of the church" and notes that a church doing missions "is fulfilling the purpose for which it was created."[3]

One way to understand that purpose is by being and building *God's* Kingdom, not our own. My own Baptist heritage owes a great deal to the fact that First Baptist Church of Boston understood this. You may recall from the first chapter how, through William Screven, FBC Boston started a Baptist church in Kittery, Maine. It was that new church that grew and, due to persecution, relocated to South Carolina. There, it grew into First Baptist Church of Charleston, the first Baptist church in the southern colonies.

A current term for a church focused on doing missions is "missional." A missional church is one that understands that God has called it out of community and is sending it into world. Further, it knows that its calling and completion of that call are possible only by the power of the Holy Spirit.

Another rich, biblical image of a missional church is that of the church as the body of Christ. Elizabeth O'Connor's 1968 book, *Journey Inward, Journey Outward,* is helpful. Breathing in and out is a natural rhythm. Missions compels a church to breathe in. When breathing in (the journey inward), the church reflects on its aims and purposes. It compares these to God's expectations. It examines its priorities and reorders them when necessary. Further, breathing in means developing budgets, organizations, and internal ministries that manifest those priorities. Like evangelism, a missional church calls, trains, incubates, and equips its members to be missionaries.

One important first step is for a church to make members aware of the many ways in which they can be involved in either career or volunteer (long- and short-term) missions work. Developing this understanding is crucial to a church's work in missions.

Then, a missional church breathes out. That is the journey outward. Simply stated, a missional church does this by sending out its members as missionaries. The first picture that comes to mind is a church commissioning individual members to go somewhere faraway to participate in some form of missions work. Many churches organize members into teams for various kinds of missions work. These projects may be local; others entail teams going on missions trips. Church members working together in a local, state, national, or international missions project *is* the church in service. That *is* the body of Christ breathing out.

For individuals, like a church, doing missions begins within, but spreads beyond ourselves. It is the result of God making a "splash" in our lives. Like a stone thrown into a pond, God moves in us and changes us. A ripple effect extends outward and, ultimately, "to the ends of the earth." With our salvation, God starts His missions work through us. Then, often when we are the most complacent, God again intervenes by calling us to serve. Our call may not be as dramatic as that of Moses. However, there may be similarities. Like Moses, we often offer excuses and tell God the reasons we are not the person to do what He is asking us to do. As it was with Moses, our call is a call to submission. In following God's leadership to serve others, a Christian acknowledges to Whom he or she belongs. In Exodus 3:4, Moses responds to God's voice out of the burning bush, "Here I am" (NASB). One Spanish Bible, the *Nueva Versión Internacional,* translates it, "Aquí me tienes." That literally means, "you have me here" or "I am yours." When we acknowledge God's call, we are saying He has us. We are His. Moses' staff was a simple tool of the trade for a shepherd like Moses. In accepting God's call to missions, Moses also yielded his staff to God's use. Similarly, to follow God in missions, we yield all we have and all we are to God's use.

Baptist Distinctives and Missions

The Authority of Scripture

Genuinely yielding to an authority means forfeiting one's options. Therefore, believing in the authority of Scripture has numerous implications for Baptist missions.

First, the authority of Scripture means missions is not an option. One obvious point of Matthew 25:31-46 and Matthew 28:18-20 is that citizens of God's Kingdom are to live as missionaries. Another is that both passages closely relate their respective commissions to Jesus' authority. It is from Jesus' throne (Matt 25:31) that He separates the sheep from the goats. Of course, in Matthew 28:18, Jesus explicitly states His authority to charge His disciples to a global missions enterprise. Further, in Matthew 5:13-16, Jesus commands us to be salt and light to the world. In verse 16, the missions purpose is clear: that the world "may see your good works, and glorify your Father who is in heaven" (NASB). To claim Scripture as authoritative in one's life is to submit to God's call to missions. Where and how one follows in the task of missions varies from person to person. Nevertheless, to reject that call is to deny with one's actions the authority of the Bible.

Second, the authority of Scripture means serving is not an option. Matthew 25:31ff makes it clear: God's people are to serve. Jesus teaches this to His disciples in Matthew 10:42-45. James 2:14-17 further shows that serving the needs of others is a natural outgrowth of faith. Again, I cannot stress enough that our service does not save us. Rather, genuine, growing faith and submission to Jesus as Lord gives rise to serving others.

Third, the authority of Scripture means choosing is not an option. This is not to suggest that any one of us can meet every human need. Throughout the Bible we find the explicit and implicit command to serve the needs that confront us. In His daily walk, Jesus encountered the blind, lame, lepers, grieving, dispossessed, outcasts, and hungry. Jesus met their needs. Through the Bible we find that we are to emulate Jesus in this way also. The needs we see will be as diverse as the people we encounter every day. They will vary as greatly as the people who live around us and throughout the world. They may be people we do not understand. They may involve situations that offend or frighten us.

Recognizing the authority of Scripture also calls us to remember a wonderful promise. In doing missions, our options may be few, but resources are available. Through the Bible God promises the greatest resource of all: His Presence. That means that whatever our task or service, God will be there to guide, strengthen, and encourage. In addition, in the Bible we find that God will also provide the human and material means by which to accomplish any assignment He gives us.

The Priesthood of All Believers

God's work in missions is done through the priesthood. First Peter 2:9-12 not only challenges God's people to function as priests; it also frames their work in terms of missions. Peter dares them to live "so that in the thing in which they slander you as evildoers, they may because of your good deeds, as they observe them, glorify God" (NASB). Peter's appeal reflects that of Jesus in Matthew 5:6 and makes one additional point. Let us put it in terms of our discussion here. When members of God's royal priesthood serve the world as God calls them, the world may say what it will and may differ greatly regarding doctrine. However, it will at least grudgingly admire them for their good deeds. In this way, the priesthood brings glory to God.

In Leviticus, the priests are set apart to minister in the contexts of both the temple and the community. The community where we live is where we first exercise and fulfill our priesthood. Our communities readily offer the familiarity that is such an important part of effective missions service. The Levites and Israelite priesthood had to learn to serve even in their community. Despite having grown up worshiping as Israelites, there were details of the priestly service that required their being trained.

Our function as a priesthood demands that we submit to similar teaching and training. And who will do the training? As happened in Israel, the training comes through other priests. Ours is a fellowship of priests training other priests for their work in missions together. This image of the partnership of priests takes seriously the gifts God has entrusted to the priesthood. At various points, we have recalled that God provides the resources to do missions service. We must also remember that one of the great assets God offers for missions are the special gifts of believers.

The General Baptists in England acknowledged the priesthood of all believers by laying hands on new converts. It was as if, after baptism, the priests were being commissioned for their missions service. Building a distinctively Baptist church through missions service requires a similar perspective.

The Autonomy of the Local Church

The local church is where the priesthood joins together as the body of Christ to serve as Jesus did. Autonomy of the local church allows each fellowship to discern for itself the needs in its community. Further, that independence means each church must also make a concerted effort to identify and evoke the gifts of its members. After all, who is in a better position for such a task than the church? Then, rather than having a missions strategy imposed, each local body is free also to explore how the abilities and capabilities God has given its members can be applied in missions service. This allows each church to connect with the real human needs in its area. From there, the church seeks further leadership from God to expand their vision as to what is their "area."

Missions is where most Baptist churches work to find a balance between autonomy and cooperation. One biblical example of churches cooperating to meet needs is the offering taken by Paul to assist those suffering famine in Judea (Acts 11:29-30). However, autonomy requires each church to choose for itself how it will model concern for all dimensions of missions service: community, state, nation, world. Most churches find that cooperation with other churches through associations, state and national conventions, and international alliances (such as the Baptist World Alliance) enhances and broadens their missions vision. Through such collaboration, missions participants can become more aware of needs throughout the world. They can also accomplish more, for all their resources—material, financial, and human—are pooled. This can enhance the whole missions process. It can make the calling, training, sending, supporting, and encouraging of missionaries more efficient and effective.

Autonomy recognizes that cooperation is really a *partnership* among churches. Partnership in missions work has been described or defined this way: "basic agreement on doctrinal/ethical issues, common goals, equality, mutual trust, submission and accountability, communication and prayer."[4] That precludes one being "over" the other, regardless of relative size or strength. It is a relationship of mutuality. It is not patronizing, but respects the genuine worth, giftedness, and autonomy of each other. It entails both independence and interdependence.

The local church has the role of nurturing, calling, and sending its members as missionaries to its community and beyond. Its autonomy frees it to choose how, when, and where—all as God leads and empowers the people.

The Ordinances of Baptism and the Lord's Supper

As we noted in the last chapter, both baptism and the Lord's Supper offer those unfamiliar with them and their meaning to ask questions. Even when language fails, the picture these rituals offer can communicate.

Understanding the symbolic nature of the ordinances allows us to be faithful to the core of their meaning while permitting varying expression within differing cultural contexts. Hence, a baptism at Villa Beach in St. Vincent (in the southern Caribbean) is no less valid than one in the Jordan River itself (where Jesus was baptized). The vast majority of Baptist churches make certain adaptations every time they observe the Lord's Supper. Most use grape juice rather than wine and small, individual cups rather than the common cup. Nor is truly unleavened bread always used. Of course, not everyone would deem all cultural accommodations regarding the ordinances appropriate. Each of us may "draw the line" in a different place. It is important for us to reconsider seriously the meaning and mode of the ordinances as revealed in Scripture.

Baptism and the Lord's Supper also serve as reminders of our call and focus. We often observe how, among other meanings, baptism is the candidate's testimony of a new relationship with Jesus. The phrase "risen to new life in Christ" is often said as the candidate is raised out of the waters of baptism. That new life involves the call to service. Therefore, we should also see baptism as the commissioning of a new missionary.

The term "Communion" is frequently used for the Lord's Supper. As an act of communion, the Lord's Supper reminds us of our common task. Jesus' broken body and shed blood—His sacrifice—*was* His service, His mission for us and our deepest need. Further, we have in common the call to follow Jesus in service. Finally, the Lord's Supper teaches us anew that we need each other to follow that call.

Religious Liberty and the Separation of Church and State

In Matthew 6:24, Jesus teaches that we cannot serve two masters. This is especially true in missions. Our missions service finds great benefit when church and state are separate. Early English Baptist leaders John Smyth and Thomas Helwys observed that the domain of civil authority is different and distinct from that of religion or the church. That people have a tremendous range of needs is obvious. We can categorize them in many ways. One is to tag them as physical, emotional, mental, and spiritual. Both church and government can address the first three. However, only the church is prepared, equipped, and called to minister to people's spiritual needs. Seldom can we effectively meet any type of need without attention to others. Therefore, churches can provide the holistic service that government cannot.

The separation of church and state also drives us to do our job. A distinctively Baptist church is free to find God's leadership because it is not compelled to service by a government. Instead, it is God who calls, convicts, commissions, equips, and sends the church to its missions task. This frees God's people to clarify their missions awareness, focus, and direction. The church is, then, free to shape missions ministry as led by God—within legal constraints. As a result, those to whom we minister are more likely to view what they are receiving as from God. And have we not found that the ultimate end of our service is to glorify God?

Separation of church and state also frees our missions effort from the stigma of church–state perceptions by governments of countries in which we may be called to minister. Unfortunately, governments among nations are often in conflict with each other. This sad reality is apparent in headlines every day. It is also one of the great causes of human misery, suffering, and need. When church and state are distinct and separate, missionaries are much less likely to be seen as agents of their country's government. Can there still be suspicion? Certainly, and there often is. But we don't expect anyone doing missions to deny her or his respective citizenship or national loyalties. Rather, we can and should submit those devotions to our citizenship in God's Kingdom.

Commitment to religious liberty and the separation of church and state keep us honest. As a testimony of our walk with God, missions should recognize rights of others and truly rely on God and not government.

In John 21:15-17, Jesus responds to Peter's declaration of love for Him with "Tend my sheep" (NASB). Jesus calls any church that would be distinctively Baptist to the same mission. Building a distinctively Baptist church in and through missions service is a daunting task. It requires that we rediscover servanthood, a virtue our culture does not highly value. It challenges our presuppositions and our pride. Doing missions service requires a humbling journey of discovery. It also demands patience, for missions takes time. William Carey, "Father of Baptist Missions" himself, worked for seven years before realizing a convert. None of us will ever see or know the ultimate end of our missions service until eternity. Then, all the glory will be to God. That is the final reason for missions, anyway.

Missions service is not "hit and run." It is a continuing matter and a never-ending task. Remember the model of the great missionary, Paul the Apostle. He, along with various companions, went out on three missionary journeys that we know of. Trace them on a map and through the book of Acts. You will find that each subsequent journey found Paul returning to locations where he had served previously. Paul spent time in those places teaching, building up, and encouraging. Also, most of Paul's letters were addressed to churches he and his partners had started and built up during their missionary journeys.

There always have been and always will be barriers to doing missions. Some are within us. Others are external. Nevertheless, Baptist distinctives allow—even challenge—Baptists to exercise the God-given and Spirit-led creativity to overcome any obstacle to serve the world in God's name.

Notes

[1] *Proceedings of the Southern Baptist Convention: Held in Augusta, Georgia, May 8th, 9th, 10th, 11th, and 12th, 1845* (Richmond VA: H. K. Ellyson, 1845), 13.

[2] Ibid., 15.

[3] William R. O'Brien, "Mission in the Valley of Postmodernity," in *Global Good News: Mission in a New Context*, ed. Howard A. Snyder (Nashville: Abingdon Press, 2001), 23.

[4] Gailyn Van Rheenen, *Missions: Biblical Foundations & Contemporary Strategies* (Grand Rapids: Zondervan, 1996), 195.

Study Questions

1. From the Bible and chapter 5, fill in the blanks in these statements about missions.

Matthew 25:31-46 teaches us that service to _____ is service

to _____.

In Matthew 5:16, Jesus teaches us that the purpose of our good works in

missions service is to _____ _____.

Matthew 25:31-46 and Matthew 28:18-20 remind us that, for disciples of

Jesus, missions service is _____.

Missions service is _____ God, _____ for

God, _____ for God, _____ for God, and

_____ for God.

2. How can our responses to God's call to service resemble that of Moses in Exodus 3?

_____

_____

_____

_____

3. What difference can God's promise of His presence make in your life of service?

_____

_____

_____

_____

4. What needs around you do you simply not understand? Do any frighten you? What can you do to overcome those barriers to service?

_____

_____

_____

_____

5. Identify the following and suggest ways your church can serve them:
• "the least of these" in your community

_____

_____

_____

_____

• "the least of these" in your state

_____

_____

_____

_____

• "the least of these" in your country

_____

_____

_____

_____

• "the least of these" in other countries

_____

_____

_____

_____

6. Consider the following: "The ways God has led Baptists (and other Christians) to serve others through missions are almost beyond number. Remember, our God who calls us to missions is the Creator. Therefore, He is creative!" What are creative ways to serve the needs of others?

_____

_____

_____

_____

Chapter 6

Building a Distinctively Baptist Church through Education

As mentioned in the previous three chapters, the church must be about the task of teaching and training its members. The late Findley Edge put it at the heart of church's identity. Edge wrote that a church should function as a minister training school or seminary. His point was that a church should always seek to prepare its members to do the work to which God calls them.[1] Paul Chaffee once observed that far too many churches fail at this: "most religious communities make too little provision for training lay leaders."[2] In this chapter, we will explore why a church trying to be distinctively Baptist cannot afford to overlook this vital function.

Most definitions of education relate to training and/or instruction. The term comes from the Latin word *educare*, which literally means "to lead out." The idea is that teaching leads the learner out of unknowing into knowing. Training also guides one from inability to ability to do something. Every culture offers some form of education or training for many differing purposes. Through practical education, the pupil might learn to hunt, farm, make pottery, cook, weave, or to do any other skill necessary for day-to-day living. On the other hand, wisdom lore would teach the person the history, morals, and values of the culture.

Those types of teaching are evident throughout the Bible. Churches are challenged to consider what skills, knowledge, and doctrines its members need to live and function as Christians today. Let's start by seeing what the Bible suggests—or commands—about the educational task of a church.

Education in the Old Testament

Education relates to knowledge. One Hebrew word, *yada*, meant "to know." It implied experience, involvement, and intimacy. A similar word was *yara*, which meant pointing out something. A related term, *torah*, meant "teaching" or "instruction." Of course, *the* Torah was the Hebrew law (and the first five books of the Old Testament). The Torah taught the Hebrews their history and was the source of their morality. It also had a practical side, guiding the training of priests and Levites for their work.

The Torah also contains the basic statement of the Hebrew faith. We know it as the *Shema* (a Hebrew word that means "hear") and find it in Deuteronomy 6:4-9. It begins, "Hear, O Israel: The Lord our God, the Lord is One" (NASB). In verse 5, it continues with what Jesus later called the Greatest Commandment (Mark 12:30-31). The command to love God includes all of one's being. It requires total commitment of the entire person. Just as God is One (undivided), so must be the faithfulness of His people. The *Shema* is a basic doctrinal statement. As importantly, it was a call for the Israelites to commit all their emotions, thoughts, and plans to God.

Verses 6-9 contain several orders regarding that commandment. God's people were to fasten these truths to their hearts. The character of God and Israel's love for God were to be in their thoughts and part of all they did.

Significant to this chapter, verse 7 is directly connected to education. It contains a direct order to teach the commands of God. In this case, teaching means more than transmitting data or information. Hebrew concepts of knowing—experience and guiding—were the basis for the teaching task of Israel.

Most of the Mosaic Law is educational in nature. Some parts give directions for the practical matters of daily life. Others involve administration of various rituals and other religious customs. Several passages address priestly training. A close study of these practical matters reveals the truths they taught Israel.

Much of the Mosaic Law deals with the feasts and festivals that Israel observed. Each was an occasion for religious instruction, and all were designed to help Israelites remember their history and heritage. We often think of remembering as recalling, or calling back to mind. Though not related etymologically, the words "remember" and "member" share an interesting visual connection. The implication of "remember" is to join with something or someone once again.

For example, the Passover celebrated God's freeing Israel from their bondage in Egypt. It included many elements, from eating unleavened bread to tasting bitter herbs. Each element reflected certain parts of the Exodus story, appealing to taste, smell, vision, and hearing. Through their senses, the Israelites could almost join with their ancestors (re-member) in the experience of God's deliverance. The Day of Atonement, as did all the sacrifices, taught the costliness of sin. The Feast of Booths (Tabernacles), reminded the Israelites about God's provision for their ancestors in the wilderness. Even the various Sabbath observances were instructive. The Sabbath day taught how God, after creating the universe, paused for refection. From observing the Sabbath year, Israel learned to be good stewards of creation. In the year of Jubilee (the Sabbath year of Sabbath years), slaves were freed, debts forgiven, and land returned to its original owner. Through this, Israel understood God's ultimate dominion, and each generation of Israel felt compelled to covenant with God as did their forebears.

Covenant, the heart of Hebrew learning and knowledge, was a matter of relationship. The first place most people learn about relationship is the home. Not surprisingly, the home was the central place of education in the Old Testament. A major, if not central, part of parental responsibility was to lead the family in faithfulness to God. The *Shema* called for religious training and education to be a natural and integral part of everyday family life. Within the family, we first experience human bonds. The same was true with Hebrew education. Children were trained in gender roles in their homes first. Fathers trained their sons to work as farmers, craftsmen, or in other ways to make a living. Mothers likewise instructed their daughters in diverse household duties and skills. Many of the skills Hebrew boys and girls learned from their parents were shaped or influenced by some aspect of the Mosaic Law. Even this practical or "vocational" training, then, had implications for religious practice.

The home and family were also places where the rituals, feasts, and festivals nurtured learning. The various elements of the Passover celebration served as object lessons and symbols as well as cues for the children to ask questions of their parents. The regular sacrifices and religious observances (such as the dietary laws) initiated family discussion. Even the functions of the priests and Levites piqued children's curiosity. The children asked questions about these observances, and the parents explained them. Learning took place.

Learning at home modeled the question/answer pattern that characterized study of the Law. It also taught a child the importance of becoming intimate with God and the story of God's covenant people. Further, this system of education taught Israel their relationship with the larger family of faith, even that of past generations.

Unfortunately, Israel was not always faithful in its covenant relationship with God. Israel was to have lived as God's special people and the object of God's love. However, they became idolaters. They began to worship the fertility gods Baal, Astarte, and others. That worship kept Israel from being what God's law had called them to be: seekers for justice and champions of the oppressed. Instead, they became oppressors of the less fortunate and perpetrators of injustice. This failure earned them God's judgment and wrath. Thus, we read in the Old Testament about others whom God sent to teach His people. These were the prophets.

When considering the prophets, many people immediately think of foretelling the future. However, the prophets actually focused on another mission. The Hebrew word most often translated "prophet" in the Old Testament is *nabhi*, which implies announcement. Some have described the Old Testament prophets as "forth-tellers" rather than foretellers. Others have explained the role of prophets as moral messengers for God. Isaiah 30:20 and 48:17 link prophets to God as Judah's Teacher. Daniel 9:10 explicitly describes the prophets as vessels of God's instruction: "nor have we obeyed the voice of the LORD our God, to walk in His teachings which He set before us through His servants the prophets" (NASB).

How prophets taught makes for an interesting study. Rich images filled the visions they received from God. These served both to illustrate the truth of God and to imprint it on the minds of the ones who saw, heard, or read the message. Prophets frequently shared object lessons in their teaching. One example is Jeremiah's use of the potter in Jeremiah 18–19. That familiar picture from daily life taught Judah of God's intention to punish them and then start over with them. Likewise, in Jeremiah 27, the prophet Jeremiah explains that God sent the people a yoke of defeat by Babylon, again using an object common to everyday life. God used Hosea's marriage as a metaphor to illustrate Israel's unfaithfulness and God's continuing attempts to redeem them. Even the names of Hosea's children taught lessons. Jezreel ("vengeance") and Lo-ruhamah ("no mercy") reminded Israel of God's impending judgment. Lo-ammi ("not my people") taught Israel the result of their disloyalty: separation from God.

The prophets' lessons of judgment were seldom devoid of hope. However, receiving hope demanded repentance. In fact, many have noted that "return" is the common theme of 8th-century BC prophets like Isaiah, Micah, Hosea, and Amos, whose ministries preceded the Babylonian Exile. Jeremiah, Ezekiel, Zechariah, and portions of Isaiah seem to reflect on punishment as past and over. These prophets, however, did teach that God's covenant people had hope—if they would live as God had taught them.

Teaching was the purpose of the Old Testament Wisdom Literature. These books—Job, Proverbs, and Ecclesiastes—were the work of the Hebrew sages. The sages were wise people from throughout Hebrew society and followed in the footsteps of Joseph. Their purpose was to consider and preserve insights regarding God and humanity. Job, for example, debates suffering and human ability to discern the working of God. Ecclesiastes explores the seeming futility of life and work. Ecclesiastes 12:13 summarizes the lesson of the entire book: "Fear God and keep his commandments, for this is the whole duty of man" (NASB). Proverbs is a collection of brief lessons by Solomon and various other sages. It underscores the emphasis placed on parental religious instruction by addressing many passages to "my son" or with stories concerning a wise (or foolish) son. Further, Proverbs speaks to many different practical matters of daily living and human conduct. Much of the Old Testament Wisdom Literature was written the form of poetry. Almost certainly, this was not an attempt to be merely appealing. Rather, it was a means by which learners could more easily remember Wisdom's lessons.

Education in the New Testament

Most of what we find related to education in the New Testament echoes that of the Old Testament. Of course, the simple explanation is that the New Testament grew out of a culture permeated by the Old Testament. Because Jesus, His disciples, and most New Testament writers were Jewish, they taught and learned the way they had been educated.

Significant for our discussion is that people often referred to Jesus Himself as "Rabbi" or "Teacher." Jesus' teaching addressed matters of concern to Jews in ways they understood. For example, in Matthew 5:17, Jesus clearly connects His teaching to that of the Old Testament: "Do not think that I have come to abolish the Law or the Prophets; I have not come to abolish them but to fulfill them" (NASB). Many Jews of Jesus' day—out of their reading of the Old Testament—were concerned with how they could recover a personal relationship with God. Jesus' answer to the question of the greatest commandment was consistent with the Old Testament teachings (Matt 22:38-40; Mark 12:28-34; Luke 10:26-28). It was also at the heart of Jesus' challenge to the "rich young ruler" of Matthew 19:16-22.

Jesus used many different methods to teach. Each was already a part of Jewish education. He used methods that helped His hearers understand and remember the lessons He taught. The parables were familiar stories and images by which they could comprehend the unfamiliar. Jesus also used puns to teach. Of course, the wordplay is often lost in translation. For example, in Matthew 23:24, Jesus refers to the scribes and Pharisees as "blind guides, who strain out a gnat and swallow a camel" (NASB). In English, we can comprehend the irony. However, it was more pronounced in the Aramaic or Hebrew of the day, in which the words for gnat (*galma*) and camel (*gamla*) are similar. Being Jewish, Jesus also used poetry and proverbs either derived from or similar to those we find in the Old Testament. Additionally, Jesus used humor to teach. Understanding more about first-century Jewish life can help us recognize more of Jesus' sense of humor. We read one instance in Luke 8:16. In that passage, Jesus says no one lights a lamp and hides it under a bed. The lamps of that time were open flames, and the beds were like cots and close to the floor. Imagine putting an open-flame lamp under a low bed. The result would surely be less light for the room. However, it would also be a very unpleasant experience for one lying on the bed! This image and the lesson were probably difficult to forget.

Jesus dealt with both the inward nature and outward expression of spirituality. In the "Sermon on the Mount" (Matt 5–7), Jesus teaches the importance of godly thoughts and feelings. However, in Matthew 5:19-20, Jesus ties the inner spiritual life to one's actions and teaches His followers to live more righteously than even the scribes and Pharisees.

Being a rabbi, Jesus had many disciples. He had an inner circle of twelve, but there were many more. Today, we call any follower of Jesus a "disciple." The Greek word translated "disciple" simply means "learner." It implies submission to and dependence on one of greater authority and knowledge. That is why the first step toward becoming a disciple is the conversion of one's attitude, mind, and heart. Only one who has been radically changed by being "born again" will appropriately submit to and depend on Jesus. Jesus requires this surrender in Matthew 16:24. It is also the core of the missional, evangelistic, and educational tasks Jesus gave us in the Great Commission.

BUILDING A DISTINCTIVELY BAPTIST CHURCH THROUGH EDUCATION

According to the commission, our educational duty is to "make disciples" by "teaching" (Matt 28:20). The Greek word for "teaching" is *didaskontes*. It implies imparting both practical and theoretical knowledge. We know that being a disciple of Jesus requires both kinds of knowledge.

One core New Testament principle about education involves all Christians. As disciples, each of us is submitted to Jesus. The result is that we teach others that they, too, may become disciples. The role of Christians is mentioned numerous times throughout the remainder of the New Testament (other than the Gospels).

Aspects of Education in a Church

Three primary factors that shape how education takes place are content, character, and curriculum. Each element influences a church's task of teaching.

Content

Content is, of course, the subject matter being taught. The content of education in a church involves both knowledge and application. There are certain issues about God, the Bible, and Christian living that we all need to understand better. Further, and more importantly, we need to live in ways that reflect that knowledge. We are to be, as James 1:22 says, doers and not just hearers of what we learn from God. Findley Edge explained the two most important goals for Bible teaching in a church as "Better Bible Knowledge" and "Better Christian Living." For Edge, the latter was primary because it was the ultimate purpose of the other.[3] That is the idea of Paul's statement in 2 Timothy 3:16-17 about the goal of Bible teaching: that people of God would be prepared for righteousness and good works. Thomas Groome put it this way: "if Christians are to live as a redeemed people, we must live in opposition to sin, both personal and social."[4] Yet another Christian writer, Charles R. Foster, has suggested that education in a church should focus on "discovering the Word-centered life," which he defines as "life founded upon the living Word of God, the written Word of God, and the proclaimed Word of God."[5]

Professional educators know we have not truly learned something until we consistently live it out. Simply stated, "If you talk the talk, you must walk the walk." A person's constancy in behavior reveals his or her convictions. Our actions are not necessarily nor absolutely in harmony with our principles. Romans 3:23 is always true. However, we should live so that others see our beliefs in our behavior.

Thus, the first task of education in a church should be to assist Christians to increase in biblical knowledge. The vital next step relates to relationships, decision, and behavior within the context of one's personal life. This way people can discover, appropriate, and apply the truths of Scripture. According to Edge, living what we learn requires churches to develop and use "all available resources."[6]

Spiritual formation is also part of the content of a church's education. In fact, it should be the guiding vision for the educational ministry of the church because it relates to our recovering spiritual direction. It both rises from and compels us to our Bible knowledge and our Christian living. It relates both to what we know and what we believe. Paul described spiritual formation well when he wrote, in Romans 12:2, "Do not conform any longer to the pattern of this world, but be transformed by the renewing of your mind" (NASB). Susanne Johnson relates it to our human ability "to recognize and to participate in God's creative and redemptive activity in all of creation."[7]

Similar to the education prescribed by the Mosaic Law, a church should also teach its history and heritage. Some question the importance of learning about the past. Those people suggest that a church should only "teach the Bible." No one would question the primacy of biblical instruction in the life of a church's educational ministry. However, there are several reasons for a church to educate its members about the past and how and why its doctrines developed.

1. *There is a biblical model.* It is not only found in the Mosaic Law. The ministries of the Old Testament prophets included calls for Israel and Judah to remember their past. Also involved was the constant reminder of the doctrine-related matter of worshipping only God.

2. *Our history and heritage are gifts.* They are the legacy left by our forebears. As seen in the first chapter, many of them suffered and many died for the beliefs, practices, and other benefits we enjoy. Doubtless, our history and heritage are also gifts from God. God inspired our forebears to see the truths that were counter to their respective cultures. God was the source of the courage they needed to endure. To fail to teach about them is poor stewardship of the gifts entrusted to us.

3. *Anything a person* truly *values is something he or she wants to share with others.* It is even more vital for the person to share with those who follow in

her or his footsteps. If such a desire does not exist, one wonders about the depth at which the person holds that belief.

4. *Any study of our history and heritage requires that we study the Bible.* Baptist history clearly shows that reverence for Scripture drove the earliest Baptists and those who followed them. The Bible was the source of their doctrine.

5. *If we do not teach our history and heritage, they will be forgotten.* Further, we will lose our identity and eventually our purpose. Teaching becomes irrelevant. Educational goals collapse. Church education becomes captive to the culture. The church's educational strategies fail.[8]

Character

The character of a church's education relates to the qualities it embodies. For Baptists in particular, see the next section relating Baptist distinctives to education. Here, I make general observations.

One quality of church education is *fellowship*. The Greek word translated "fellowship" in the New Testament is *koinonia*. Acts 2:42, 1 Corinthians 1:9, and 2 Corinthians 13:14 are three examples of verses containing this word. Fellowship is more than punch and cookies after church on Sunday night. The concept involves things we hold in common. In education, it stresses genuine dialogue as a central method. True conversation grows out of fellowship. This, in turn, creates appreciation and further communication despite the many social differences that can exist among church members.

Church education must be *prophetic*. Being prophetic requires the equipping of church members to be messengers for God in today's world. This means church education should develop thinking, empowered, and rooted people. Education in a church should help members learn to reflect on current events, enabling them to anticipate how Bible knowledge can speak to contemporary needs. Fads and trends come and go, but church education keeps the consistency of biblical relevance in the forefront. Church members need to learn how to avoid following the current craze, which can lead to unwitting violation of basic principles.

Education in a church should also be *intentional* and *purposeful*. It is said, "If you aim at nothing, that is what you will hit." This is true with education. There are simply too many needs to address, too many things to teach and learn, and too much to know for education to be haphazard. A church must develop goals for its educational task. Then it must develop a "road map" to get to that destination. Finally, it must follow that map.

Education within a church must also be *creative*. Leaders must be aware of and sensitive to the differences that exist among church members/learners. One of the greatest differences found in most churches relates to developmental issues. How we learn and what we need change radically from childhood to adolescence, to adulthood, to senior adulthood. For example, how can a church effectively heed Jesus' call for His disciples to allow children access to Him? (Matt 19:14). Keeping in mind that religious language is symbolic and that children think concretely, churches need to teach biblical stories and precepts in ways that take children's learning styles into account. Adults, on the other hand, are able to think abstractly and to examine complex ideas. Teaching people of all ages and backgrounds in terms they can understand establishes the pattern of accepting people "where they are." Designing and implementing such strategies require creativity.

In everything it does, church education should be *redemptive*. First, we know God wishes to redeem all people (John 3:16). This means everyone needs to learn about God. First Corinthians 13:12 indicates that there will always be more for everyone to learn. Learning continues as the church teaches all people "the depth of the riches both of the wisdom and knowledge of God" (Rom 11:33, NASB). That is quite a "tall order." However, to be redemptive implies that no person—regardless of age, social position, or level of education—is beyond learning about God. Whether an infant, a developmentally disabled individual, or a "typical" youth or adult, each person can learn *something* about God. It may be as simple as experiencing God's love through another. It could be as profound as the Trinity of God. Church education must focus on using the available opportunities, gifts, and resources to teach creatively.

Curriculum

We often think of a church's curriculum as the printed material it uses in teaching—quarterlies, learning and teaching guides, etc. Sometimes we think of curriculum in terms of the church's classes, organizations, events, and ministries designed for the overt purpose of education.

However, curriculum is usually defined as courses directed toward a common goal of a given educational organization. In those basic terms, then, everything the church does is its curriculum. That includes the church's worship, evangelism, and missions service. Each one of those aspects of church life and work teaches more than we realize. (Of course, as we have seen in the preceding chapters, each also requires education.)

Maria Harris describes three types of church curricula: the implicit, the explicit, and the null.[9] Let's look briefly at how each is expressed in the context of a local church.

The *explicit curriculum* is what the church intends, plans, and works to teach. Many churches develop missions or vision statements. These serve the purpose of guiding a church in its work so that it actually does what it says it intends to do. All the ministries a church uses to accomplish its mission or vision *are* that church's explicit curriculum or, at least, parts of it.

Each church also teaches many things by implication. One way to discover a church's *implicit curriculum* is by looking at its organizations, budget, and calendar. For example, many churches state that they intend to teach their members missions awareness, missions support, and missions service. However, what if a church has a budget that allocates only miniscule to missions? What if its calendar shows little time for missions education? What can we infer? What is that church really teaching? We can ask the same questions about the way a church accomplishes its tasks. That, too, is part of the church's implicit curriculum.

The *null curriculum* is what a church teaches by simply leaving something out. For example, what does a church teach by never mentioning evangelism and never planning, training, or scheduling opportunities for it? By paying it no heed, that church's null curriculum teaches the irrelevancy or unimportance of evangelism.

Baptist Distinctives and Education

The Authority of Scripture

The authority of Scripture should permeate everything a distinctively Baptist church does in education. Most obvious is that the Bible is the foundation and must shape all aspects of a church's teaching: content, character, and curriculum. After all, we have already discussed how Bible knowledge is the first step toward the ultimate goal of education in the church: the goal of Christian living.

Also apparent is that biblical authority requires ethical, cultural, and developmental relevance in church teaching. Second Timothy 3:16-17 demands practical application of our Bible study and teaching. Hebrews 4:12 adds, "For the word of God is living and active and sharper than any two-edged sword, and piercing as far as the division of soul and spirit, of both joints and marrow, and able to judge the thoughts and intentions of the heart" (NASB). This makes it vital that a church's Bible teaching links biblical precepts written in the Middle East more than 2,000 years ago to the needs and situations of people today and, potentially, anywhere. The basic issues remain the same. However, the manifestations differ tremendously. Further, a church must educate in Scripture not only to meet people's needs, but also in ways and with vocabulary and concepts they understand. Of course, identifying those needs, the vocabulary, and the concepts that will make sense to the learners means that the teachers must understand the culture of the community or demographic they wish to reach.

Since the authority of Scripture extends to every area of a person's moral, ethical, and spiritual life, a church must teach in ways consistent with the learners' developmental capacities. As described earlier in regard to principles of education, this means teaching a child as a child, an adolescent as an adolescent, and an adult as an adult is not only a wise and commonsense approach to education. It is also yet another expression of a church's regard for biblical authority.

One obvious impact of biblical authority on education is easily overlooked. If we believe that the Bible matters and that all people have the right to read and interpret it for themselves, they must be able to read the Bible. Baptist churches should be on the forefront of literacy training, teaching English as a second language (ESL), and supporting Bible translation ministries. A distinctively Baptist church will view these ministries as central to their work and not as secondary activities.

We must take our study and interpretation of the Bible seriously. A distinctively Baptist church teaches learners how to interpret the Bible for themselves, even what they hear in sermons. This is not to suggest that they not believe or trust their pastors or others who preach. Rather, they must listen with open hearts to what God says both directly and through the preacher. This is a sobering task. However, it is one to which the Bible calls us. For instance, 1 Thessalonians 5:19-21 tells us, "Do not quench the Spirit; do not despise prophetic utterances. But examine everything carefully; hold fast to that which is good" (NASB).

The call of 2 Timothy 2:15 is always to "accurately" and "correctly" interpret the Bible and apply it to our lives. Knowledge of the Bible's geography and its historical and cultural backgrounds enhances our understanding of Scripture. Teaching those and encouraging learners to be more aware of contemporary issues and events are ways a church can equip its members for their task of biblical interpretation.

We find one of the most important principles of biblical interpretation in Hebrews 12:2: "fixing our eyes on Jesus, the author and perfecter of faith" (NASB). The 1963 *Baptist Faith and Message* applies that verse to interpretation this way: "The criterion by which the Bible is to be interpreted is Jesus Christ."[10] The 2000 *Baptist Faith and Message* statement omits that phrase.

The Priesthood of All Believers

Education is essential for Christians to function most effectively in their priesthood. The preceding paragraphs show how Christians can and should be taught for their work of "accurately handling the word of truth" (2 Tim 2:15, NASB).

Our respective ministries and gifts need skill training that can make our service more effective. Simply having a gift does not necessarily mean one is ready to perform a task well, whether the task is volunteering for a service project, helping in the church kitchen, chairing a committee, or teaching a Sunday school class. Of course, there are countless other tasks in all churches, and church members willing to do those tasks need training in order to perform them. If they are not trained, they are not likely to do their jobs well, or they may become frustrated and quit. An education ministry that involves equipping the priesthood with the skills for their tasks is likely to avoid those problems.

The priesthood of all believers encourages students and teachers to see themselves as partners in learning. It encourages them to be fellow pilgrims as they study together and apply what they learn to the community and world. The mutuality of the priesthood engenders relationships of service, acceptance, and accountability. Based on these bonds, learning becomes more relevant to believers' lives, needs, and gifts.

In and through its educational ministry, a church takes seriously the importance of each member's priestly function regardless of age. Through education, a distinctively Baptist church challenges, equips, nurtures, and enables all its members for their roles as priests. This requires training and teaching to be sensitive to the respective developmental level and gifts of every member. Such awareness calls all churches and church members to greater intimacy and deeper fellowship.

The church that so educates, equips, and empowers its members in their individual ministries will be the greatest expression of what it means to be Baptist. It will also see God do great things in and through its members.

The Autonomy of the Local Church

The local church is the primary place where Christian education occurs. The fellowship that exists within the family of faith is vital to learning. Further, all churches have the essential purpose of educating their members toward God.

Only if a church is free to decide and design for itself the content, character, curriculum, and teachers of its educational ministry can it become a place where members feel secure enough to explore areas of their lives that can be intimidating. Only the local church can know itself well enough to provide a fellowship where members feel safe enough to examine the depths of their personhood and their relationships with others and God. Each church, as a family of faith, also functions as a guide to this intimacy, openness, and acceptance. For those qualities to be genuine, the church must be free and independent.

Autonomy also allows each church to respond to its unique educational needs and tasks. The individual church best knows the details and specific nature of the programs and ministries necessary to fulfill its mission. It also best knows what gifts exist among its members that can help accomplish those tasks successfully. Can a local church need or use external consultants? Certainly. Many people and organizations understand general issues related to the many dimensions of Christian education. Local churches can—and often should—consult those kinds of resources as they design and carry out their ministries of education. However, each church must be free to make and implement those decisions in light of its particular situation.

Those specifics may involve many different issues that influence education. Educational technologies available to churches vary greatly. Diverse cultures require different and creative approaches to teaching. Therefore, each church must be free to choose forms, materials, teachers, leaders by and through which it will teach. Each church should take both its autonomy and its educational task seriously.

The Ordinances of Baptism and the Lord's Supper

Both ordinances have similar educational roles as did the feasts and festivals commanded by Mosaic Law. Both portray important events. Of course, baptism reenacts Jesus' own baptism. These ordinances' respective images teach Christians by reminding them and calling them to join once again with Jesus' story and their own initial experiences with Him. They also teach non-Christians by offering initial awareness in visual images.

A distinctively Baptist church can also use the ordinances as occasions to teach about Baptist beliefs. Simple, brief explanations about an ordinance remind Christian observers of its meaning and importance. For observers new to the ordinances, such explanations clarify what is unfamiliar to them.

Both ordinances are also opportunities for Christians to exercise their individual priestly function through education. In baptism, the candidate teaches through his or her testimony either through spoken confession of faith or the baptism itself. A church can offer the chance for candidates' further or deeper participation by allowing them input regarding the development and design of their baptism. Educational activities should be creative.

Likewise, the Lord's Supper affords many means to involve the laity. Most Baptist churches assign their deacons the task of assisting the pastor in distributing the bread and wine. Passing the elements person to person is an image of the members functioning as priests by serving each other. During the Lord's Supper, members usually are led to reflect inwardly on its meaning. A church trying to be more distinctively Baptist may also want to invite some members to share their reflections with those around them or the rest of the congregation.

The ordinances are vital symbols as well as acts of obedience. A distinctively Baptist church recognizes their educational potential. It then employs creativity to plan and act accordingly.

Religious Liberty and the Separation of Church and State

A church must be free to design and implement its ministry of education within its own doctrinal and traditional limits. Religious liberty and the separation of church and state provide this freedom. It also provides the opportunity for a church to do its work free from external impositions. The boundaries this separation offers leaves to each church the creation of and implementation of curriculum, content, methods, and teachers in its education. The government decides none of this. The result is that the content and character of education differs from church to church. Christian education is unique as each church brings its theology and practice to bear on its individual context and culture. However, that same freedom requires a distinctively Baptist church to teach its tenets and respect the rights of others to teach theirs within the same constraints.

As was true related to the preceding chapters, religious liberty and the separation of church and state clarifies for churches their job in education. Just as it is the church's, not the state's, responsibility to evangelize, so it is regarding education. It is the church's—and the family's—job to teach the Bible and prayer, not the government's job through schools. That is why government-mandated prayers are not allowed in U.S. public schools. This does not forbid prayer or Bible reading not imposed on others. Rather, it actually frees anyone to pray or read the Bible at school—again as long as it is not counter to classroom activities or forced on others. Nor can the same be imposed on any of us in public life. After all, many "good Baptists" would feel uncomfortable being expected or coerced to join in a prayer led by a Muslim or other non-Christian. Here again, our Lord's command in the Golden Rule requires us to act accordingly when those roles are reversed.

The freedom allowed by the separation of church and state reminds us of the nature of faith. A Baptist church's education must always allow for learners freely to study and explore as God leads and speaks to them. Only by this freedom can students genuinely learn and apply biblical truths to their lives.

A church wishing to be genuinely and distinctively Baptist will take seriously all it does to teach. It will plan its own work deliberately and use every legitimate opportunity to teach and train its members to do their work. Further, it will do its own work freely and creatively and not leave the task to any other body.

Notes

[1] Findley B. Edge, *The Greening of the Church* (Waco TX: Word Books, Publisher, 1971), 179.

[2] Paul Chaffee, *Accountable Leadership: A Resource Guide for Sustaining Legal, Financial, and Ethical Integrity in Today's Congregations* (San Francisco: Jossey-Bass, 1997), xiv.

[3] Findley B. Edge, *Teaching for Results*, rev. ed. (Nashville: Broadman & Holman, 1995), 4.

[4] Thomas H. Groome, *Christian Religious Education: Sharing Our Story and Vision* (San Francisco: Harper & Row, Publishers, 1980), 94.

[5] Charles R. Foster, *Educating Congregations: The Future of Christian Education* (Nashville: Abingdon Press, 1994), 233.

[6] Findley B. Edge, *A Quest for Vitality in Religion: A Theological Approach to Religious Education*, rev. ed. (Macon GA: Smyth & Helwys Publishing, 1994), 83.

[7] Susanne Johnson, *Christian Spiritual Formation in the Church and Classroom* (Nashville: Abingdon Press, 1989), 22.

[8] Foster, *Educating Congregations,* 22-35.

[9] Maria Harris, *Fashion Me a People: Curriculum in the Church* (Louisville KY: Westminster/John Knox Press, 1989), 68-69.

[10] *The Baptist Faith and Message* (Nashville: The Sunday School Board of the Southern Baptist Convention, 1963), 7.

Study Questions

A. *Education in the Mosaic Law*
Fill in the blanks with the appropriate phrase from the list below.

1. The Feast of Passover taught the Hebrews about

_____.

2. The Feast of Tabernacles taught the Hebrews about

_____.

3. The Day of Atonement taught the Hebrews about

_____.

4. The Sabbath day taught the Hebrews about

_____.

5. The Sabbath year taught the Hebrews about

_____.

6. The Jubilee year taught the Hebrews about

_____.

God's creative activity and His pausing for reflection
God's deliverance from bondage in Egypt
Stewardship of creation
God's provision for Israel in the wilderness
God's ultimate dominion
The costliness of sin

B. Lessons from the Prophets
Describe two object lessons as described in this chapter used by each of these prophets and the lesson each method was meant to teach.

1. Jeremiah

_____

_____

_____

_____

2. Hosea

_____

_____

_____

_____

C. Lessons from Old Testament Wisdom Literature
Write the name of the book of Old Testament Wisdom Literature (Job, Proverbs, Ecclesiastes) after the phrase that best describes it.

1. This book teaches about the seeming futility of life and work.

_____

2. This book teaches about suffering and human ability to discern the working of God. _____

3. This book teaches about many practical matters of daily living and human conduct. _____

Additional Questions

1. In the New Testament, Jesus is most often referred to by the Jewish title

_____, which means _____.

2. List three of Jesus' teaching methods mentioned in the book.

_____

_____

_____

_____

3. What do each of the following passages suggest about the need for the Bible and a church's education ministry?

• 2 Timothy 2:15

_____

_____

_____

• 2 Timothy 3:16-17

_____

_____

_____

• Hebrews 12:2

_____

_____

_____

• Hebrews 4:12

_____

_____

_____

4. How well is your church's education ministry characterized by each of the
   following terms?

• Fellowship

_____

_____

_____

• Prophetic

_____

_____

_____

• Intentional

_____

_____

_____

• Creative

_____

_____

_____

• Redemptive

_____

_____

_____

5. What were other ways Jesus taught?

_____

_____

_____

6. How do your church's worship, evangelism, and missions service teach?

_____

_____

_____

_____

7. What is your church's stated curriculum?

_____

_____

_____

_____

8. What do your church's budget and calendar say about your church's educational goals?

_____

_____

_____

_____

9. How well are Baptist distinctives included in the content of your church's education ministry?

_____

_____

_____

_____

10. What are some specific ways your church's education ministry reflects each Baptist distinctive studied in the book? How can that improve?

_____

_____

_____

_____

Appendix

The following list includes additional resources for studying Baptist history and distinctives.

Recommended Nonfiction

Brackney, William H. editor. *Baptist Life and Thought: A Source Book.* Revised edition. Valley Forge PA: Judson Press, 1998. This is a collection of excerpts from important documents in Baptist history with helpful historical notes. A good addition to a church library for those wishing to read original documents.

Estep, William R. *Why Baptists? A Study of Baptist Faith and Heritage.* Dallas: Baptist General Convention of Texas, 1997. As the title suggests, this is an examination of Baptist history and the development of Baptist doctrines. Intended for use in a local church.

Fletcher, Jesse C. *The Southern Baptist Convention: A Sesquicentennial History.* Nashville: Broadman & Holman, 1994. An excellent history that focuses on this specific Baptist group. Thorough and scholarly; communicates well to laity.

Helwys, Thomas. *A Short Declaration of the Mystery on Iniquity.* Classics of Religious Liberty 1. Edited and introduced by Richard Groves. Macon GA: Mercer University Press, 1998. This is the work of Helwys cited in my first chapter above. It is interesting reading for those who want to study the context and form of Helwys's thoughts.

Leonard, Bill J. *Baptist Ways: A History.* Valley Forge PA: Judson Press, 2003. Well-written and comprehensive Baptist history that speaks to a broad readership—both scholars and laity alike.

McBeth, H. Leon. *The Baptist Heritage: Four Centuries of Baptist Witness.* Nashville: Broadman, 1987. This Baptist comprehensive history is scholarly, but helpful when used as an encyclopedia.

———. *A Source Book for Baptist Heritage.* Nashville: Broadman, 1990. This is an extensive collection of lengthy excerpts from documents throughout Baptist history with helpful historical notes. Another good addition to a church library for those wishing to read original documents.

Shurden, Walter B. *The Baptist Identity: Four Fragile Freedoms.* Macon GA: Smyth & Helwys, 1993. This small book is an excellent overview of basic Baptist doctrines and the freedom found in each. It is an introduction to the "Proclaiming the Baptist Vision" series edited by Shurden and published by Smyth & Helwys.

Williams, Roger. *The Bloudy Tenent of Persecution, for Cause of Conscience Discussed in a Conference between Truth and Peace.* Edited by Richard Groves. Introduced by Edwin Gaustad. Macon GA: Mercer University Press, 2001. Roger Williams wrote *The Bloudy Tenent of Persecution* in 1644. Many consider it his most important writing and a classic in the development of Baptist history and doctrine. In this edition, the editor establishes the historical context in which Williams lived and wrote and mentions Roger Williams's other writings. Williams's seventeenth-century writing style makes the book a bit difficult for some readers. However, many laypeople would appreciate reading directly what Williams thought.

Recommended Fiction

Will Campbell, Baptist minister-at-large, lives in Mt. Juliet, Tennessee. He has written two novels that especially address the heart and emotion of what makes one Baptist.

The Glad River (1982; repr., Macon GA: Smyth & Helwys, 2005) traces the growing friendship of three young men, fellow pilgrims in life and faith. One, Doops Momber, is a budding writer searching for "a real Baptist." This novel is interspersed with excerpts from a novel about Baptists that the character Doops is writing.

Originally published in 1983, *Cecelia's Sin: A Novella* (Macon GA: Mercer University Press, 1993) is somewhat of a sequel to *The Glad River.* In it Campbell completes the novel begun by Doops Momber about the struggles of Anabaptists in Amsterdam. The introduction to the book, "Birth of the Baptist Movement," by Eric W. Gritsch, is a brief but helpful summary of early Baptist history.

Periodicals and Journals

Baptists Today
P.O. Box 6318
Macon, GA 31208-6318
1-877-752-5658

"*Baptists Today* serves churches by providing a reliable source of unrestricted news coverage, thoughtful analysis and inspiring features focusing on issues of importance to Baptist Christians." (from *Baptists Today* 25/3 [March 2007]: 3)

Christian Ethics Today
Christian Ethics Today Foundation
9608 Parkview Court
Denton, TX 76207
(940) 262-0450

Heritage Seekers (HeritageSeekers.org)
Heritage Seekers is a magazine designed to teach children about Baptist history and heritage. It is published by The Center for Baptist Heritage & Studies in Richmond, Virginia. The magazine is user- and family-friendly and can be used in churches in numerous ways.

Web Sites for Baptist History and Heritage *(all information is current and correct as of November 6, 2007)*
Associated Baptist Press
www.abpnews.com
ABP covers issues of national and international importance to Baptists.

Baptist Faith & Message
www.bgct.org/TexasBaptists/Document.Doc?&id=610
This page is found on the Web site of the Baptist General Convention of Texas. It is especially helpful in comparing and contrasting the 1963 and 2000 *Baptist Faith and Message* statements.

Baptist Joint Committee
http://www.bjconline.org
Supported by individual Baptists, local Baptist churches, and fourteen Baptist bodies, the Baptist Joint Committee has long been a Baptist witness to all three branches of the United States government. This statement is from the BJC Web site: "The mission of the Baptist Joint Committee for Religious Liberty is to defend and extend God-given religious liberty for all, furthering the Baptist heritage that champions the principle that religion must be freely exercised, neither advanced nor inhibited by government." The BJC website is an excellent resource for information on the history of

and need for religious liberty and separation of church and state and current events/issues relating to that Baptist distinctive.

Baptist History & Heritage Society
www.baptisthistory.org
Mission statement: "Helping Baptists discover, conserve, assess, and share their history."
This is an independent organization supported mostly by membership dues from individual Baptists, Baptist colleges and universities, state conventions, and churches. It sponsors annual meetings and is a superb resource for printed and online material about Baptist history. The Web site has a catalog for ordering materials. The society also publishes the *Baptist History and Heritage Journal* (subscription information is available on the Web site).

Baptist World Alliance
http://www.bwanet.org
Mentioned in the first chapter of the book, the BWA is comprised of more than two hundred Baptist bodies from around the globe and supported by numerous individual Baptists. The BWA and its Web site offer resources as well as opportunities to network and serve with Baptists around the world. The following is the group's vision statement (from the BWA Web site): "The Baptist World Alliance is a global movement of Baptists sharing a common confession of faith in Jesus Christ, bonded together by God's love to support, encourage and strengthen one another, while proclaiming and living the Gospel of Jesus Christ in the power of the Holy Spirit to a lost world."

BaptistLife.com
http://www.baptistlife.com
This Web site provides online networking with and information on many different Baptist groups. It has links to various Baptist publications and news sources.

Baptistnet
http://www.baptistnet.com

EthicsDaily.com
http://www.baptists4ethics.com

A Web site developed by Baptists with information and printed and audio-visual resources to inform Baptists on ethical issues. It has a good section on Baptist history. The "Curricula" section offers excellent lessons one can order for use in one's church.

Smyth & Helwys Publishing
www.helwys.com
Smyth & Helwys publishes a full range of books, Sunday school curriculum, and Bible studies. Offerings include various books on Baptist history and doctrine, especially the series *Proclaiming the Baptist Vision*, in which each short book focuses on a respective Baptist distinctive. Each book is a collection of articles, sermons, and essays written by leaders, ministers, laity, and scholars from across the spectrum of Baptist life. The varying perspectives challenge the reader to deeper reflection on Baptist distinctives.

Virginia Baptist Historical Society and the Center for Baptist Heritage and Studies
http://www.baptistheritage.org/
From the Web site: "Established in 2000 following an agreement between the Baptist General Association of Virginia, the University of Richmond and the Virginia Baptist Historical Society, the Center for Baptist Heritage & Studies seeks to champion Baptist distinctives and Baptist heritage and to provide educational opportunities related to Baptist distinctives, history and heritage. It accomplishes its mission in numerous ways, including making available Baptist records and historical materials and through serving as a research and resource center. The Center offers academic and special interest courses through the School of Continuing Studies at the University of Richmond. The Center also presents lectures, seminars, and workshops."

1, 2, 3 John and Jude (Annual Bible Study series)
Learning and Living the Truth
Judson Edwards

Studying these four letters will challenge readers to consider their own truth—the truth that governs their lives and the truth they feel is worth living and dying for. In a world where truth is a slippery reality, 1, 2, 3 John and Jude remind us that truth does exist and that truth still sets people free. *Teaching Guide 978-1-57312-982-4 152 pages/pb* **$14.00**

Study Guide 978-1-57312-983-1 92 pages/pb **$6.00**

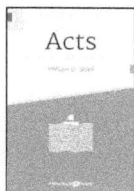

Acts (Preaching the Word Series)
William D. Shiell

In this collection of sermons on the book of Acts, William Shiell examines the disciples' efforts as they learned to share the gospel and foster character formation and fellowship. Shiell reveals how the resurrection of Jesus and the power of the Spirit disrupted cities across the Mediterranean—and how this message and Power are still capable of "turning the world upside down." *978-1-57312-906-0 234 pages/pb* **$18.00**

Atonement in the Apocalypse
An Exposé of the Defeat of Evil
Robert W. Canoy

Revelation calls believers to see themselves through the unique lens of redemptive atonement and to live and model daily that they see themselves in the present moment as redeemed people. Having thus seen themselves, believers likewise are directed to see and to relate to others in this world the very way that God has seen them from eternity.

978-1-57312-946-6 218 pages/pb **$22.00**

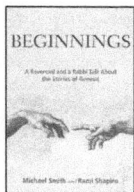

Beginnings
A Reverend and a Rabbi Talk About the Stories of Genesis
Michael Smith and Rami Shapiro

Editor Aaron Herschel Shapiro declares that stories "must be retold—not just repeated, but reinvented, reimagined, and reexperienced" to remain vital in the world. Mike and Rami continue their conversations from the *Mount and Mountain* books, exploring the places where their traditions intersect and diverge, listening to each other as they respond to the stories of Genesis. *978-1-57312-772-1 202 pages/pb* **$18.00**

Bugles in the Afternoon
Dealing with Discouragement and Disillusionment in Ministry
Judson Edwards

In *Bugles in the Afternoon*, Edwards writes, "My long experience in the church has convinced me that most ministers—both professional and lay—spend time under the juniper tree. Those ministers who have served more than ten years and not been depressed, discouraged, or disillusioned can hold their annual convention in a phone booth."

978-1-57312-865-0 148 pages/pb **$16.00**

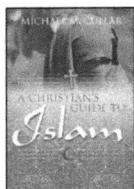

A Christian's Guide to Islam
Michael D. McCullar

A *Christian's Guide to Islam* provides a brief but accurate guide to Muslim formation, history, structure, beliefs, practices, and goals. It explores to what degree the tenets of Islam have been misinterpreted, corrupted, or abused over the centuries.

978-1-57312-512-3 128 pages/pb **$16.00**

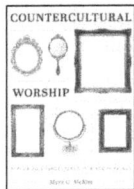

Countercultural Worship
A Plea to Evangelicals in a Secular Age
Mark G. McKim

Evangelical worship, McKim argues, has drifted far from both its biblical roots and historic origins, leaving evangelicals in danger of becoming mere chaplains to the wider culture, oblivious to the contradictions between what the secular culture says is real and important and what Scripture says is real and important.

978-1-57312-873-5 174 pages/pb **$19.00**

Crisis Ministry: A Handbook
Daniel G. Bagby

Covering more than 25 crisis pastoral care situations, this book provides a brief, practical guide for church leaders and other caregivers responding to stressful situations in the lives of parishioners. It tells how to resource caregiving professionals in the community who can help people in distress.

978-1-57312-370-9 154 pages/pb **$15.00**

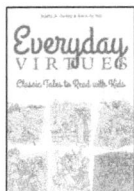

Everyday Virtues
Classic Tales to Read with Kids
James A. Autry & Rick Autry

This book of stories collected by a father and grandfather team invites adults and children to read together. Featuring the six virtues of justice, humility, courage, compassion, freedom, and respect, these entertaining and easily understood stories from all over the world focus on what makes us truly human.

978-1-57312-971-8 220 pages/pb **$18.00**

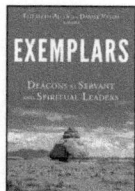

Exemplars
Deacons as Servant and Spiritual Leaders
Elizabeth Allen and Daniel Vestal, eds.

Who Do Deacons Need to Be? What Do Deacons Need to Know? What Do Deacons Need to Do? These three questions form the basis for *Exemplars: Deacons as Servant and Spiritual Leaders*. They are designed to encourage robust conversation within diaconates as well as between deacons, clergy, and other laity.   *978-1-57312-876-6 128 pages/pb* **$15.00**

Faith, Hope & Politics
Inspiring a New Generation to Community-Changing Political Engagement
Brent McDougal

Through personal narrative, stories of inspiration, and a deep dive into fifteen qualities future leaders will need to make a lasting impact, Brent McDougal challenges the next generation to give their lives to a more hopeful and just future—a future in which faith, hope, and love have the power to transform America.   *978-1-57312-992-3 174 pages/pb* **$18.00**

Five Hundred Miles
Reflections on Calling and Pilgrimage
Lauren Brewer Bass

Spain's Camino de Santiago, the Way of St. James, has been a cherished pilgrimage path for centuries, visited by countless people searching for healing, solace, purpose, and hope. These stories from her five-hundred-mile-walk is Lauren Brewer Bass's honest look at the often winding, always surprising journey of a calling.   *978-1-57312-812-4 142 pages/pb* **$16.00**

A Five-Mile Walk
Exploring Themes in the Experience of Christian Faith and Discipleship
Michael B. Brown

Sometimes the Christian journey is a stroll along quiet shores. Other times it is an uphill climb on narrow, snow-covered mountain paths. Usually, it is simply walking in the direction of wholeness, one step after another, sometimes even two steps forward and one step back.

978-1-57312-852-0 196 pages/pb **$18.00**

Glimpses from State Street
Wayne Ballard

As a collection of devotionals, *Glimpses from State Street* provides a wealth of insights and new ways to consider and develop our fellowship with Christ. It also serves as a window into the relationship between a small town pastor and a welcoming congregation.

978-1-57312-841-4 158 pages/pb **$15.00**

To order call **1-800-747-3016** or visit **www.helwys.com**

God's Servants, the Prophets
Bryan Bibb

God's Servants, the Prophets covers the Israelite and Judean prophetic literature from the preexilic period. It includes Amos, Hosea, Isaiah, Micah, Zephaniah, Nahum, Habakkuk, Jeremiah, and Obadiah.

978-1-57312-758-5 208 pages/pb **$16.00**

Holy Hilarity
A Funny Study of Genesis
Mark Roncace

Mark Roncace brings readers fifty-three short chapters of wit and amusing observations about the biblical stories, followed by five thought-provoking questions for individual reflection or group discussion. Humorous, yet reverent, this refreshing approach to Bible study invites us, whatever our background, to wrestle with the issues in the text and discover the ways those issues intersect our own messy lives. *978-157312-892-6 230 pages/pb* **$17.00**

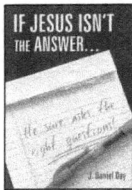

If Jesus Isn't the Answer . . . He Sure Asks the Right Questions!
J. Daniel Day

Taking eleven of Jesus' questions as its core, Day invites readers into their own conversation with Jesus. Equal parts testimony, theological instruction, pastoral counseling, and autobiography, the book is ultimately an invitation to honest Christian discipleship.

978-1-57312-797-4 148 pages/pb **$16.00**

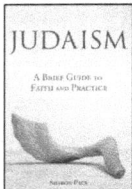

Judaism
A Brief Guide to Faith and Practice
Sharon Pace

Sharon Pace's newest book is a sensitive and comprehensive introduction to Judaism. How does belief in the One God and a universal morality shape the way in which Jews see the world? How does one find meaning in life and the courage to endure suffering? How does one mark joy and forge community ties? *978-1-57312-644-1 144 pages/pb* **$16.00**

Live the Stories
50 Interactive Children's Sermons
Andrew Noe

Live the Stories provides church leaders a practical guide to teaching children during the worship service through play—and invites the rest of the congregation to join the fun. Noe's lessons allow children to play, laugh, and act out the stories of our faith and turn the sanctuary into a living testimony to what God has done in the past, is doing in the present, and will do in the future. *978-1-57312-943-5 128 pages/pb* **$14.00**

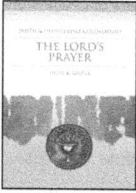

The Lord's Prayer (Smyth & Helwys Bible Commentary Supplemental Series)
Nijay K. Gupta

The Lord's Prayer is the most recited, most memorized, and most studied text in the Bible. It also contains several conundrums: what does it mean to "hallow" the Father's name? What relationship does our forgiveness of others have with God's forgiveness for us? If God does not tempt, why would we pray "Lead us not into temptation"? This commentary not only addresses these important questions but also offers insight into how the global church throughout generations has interacted with the Lord's Prayer and has found in it inspiration and hope.   *978-1-57312-984-8 200 pages/hc* **$40.00**

Loyal Dissenters
Reading Scripture and Talking Freedom with 17th-century English Baptists
Lee Canipe

When Baptists in 17th-century England wanted to talk about freedom, they unfailingly began by reading the Bible—and what they found in Scripture inspired their compelling (and, ultimately, successful) arguments for religious liberty. In an age of widespread anxiety, suspicion, and hostility, these early Baptists refused to worship God in keeping with the king's command.   *978-1-57312-872-8 178 pages/pb* **$19.00**

Meditations on Luke
Daily Devotions from the Gentile Physician
Chris Cadenhead

Readers searching for a fresh encounter with Scripture can delve into *Meditations on Luke*, a collection of daily devotions intended to guide the reader through the book of Luke, which gives us some of the most memorable stories in all of Scripture. The Scripture, response, and prayer will guide readers' own meditations as they listen and respond to God's voice, coming to us through Luke's Gospel.   *978-1-57312-947-3 328 pages/pb* **$22.00**

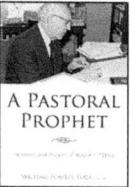

A Pastoral Prophet
Sermons and Prayers of Wayne E. Oates
William Powell Tuck, ed.

Read these sermons and prayers and look directly into the heart of Wayne Oates. He was a consummate counselor, theologian, and writer, but first of all he was a pastor. . . . He gave voice to our deepest hurts, then followed with words we long to hear: you are not alone.

—Kay Shurden
Associate Professor Emeritus, Clinical Education,
Mercer University School of Medicine, Macon, Georgia
978-157312-955-8 160 pages/pb **$18.00**

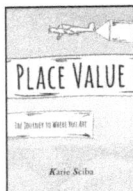

Place Value
The Journey to Where You Are
Katie Sciba

Does a place have value? Can a place change us? Is it possible for God to use the place you are in to form you? From Victoria, Texas to Indonesia, Belize, Australia, and beyond, Katie Sciba's wanderlust serves as a framework to understand your own places of deep emotion and how God may have been weaving redemption around you all along.

978-157312-829-2 138 pages/pb **$15.00**

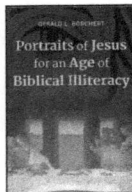

Portraits of Jesus
for an Age of Biblical Illiteracy
Gerald L. Borchert

Despite our era of communication and information overload, biblical illiteracy is widespread. In *Portraits of Jesus*, Gerald L. Borchert assists both ministers and laypeople with a return to what the New Testament writers say about this stunning Jesus who shocked the world and called a small company of believers into an electrifying transformation.

978-157312-940-4 212 pages/pb **$20.00**

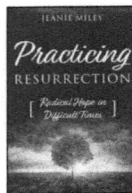

Practicing Resurrection
Radical Hope in Difficult Times
Jeanie Miley

Through stories of her own literal and metaphorical journeys toward hope and renewal, Miley demonstrates that when we face hardship or the inevitable, difficult transitions in life, we may *practice resurrection*—and trust steadily in the goodness and mercy of God.

978-1-57312-972-5 218 pages/pb **$19.00**

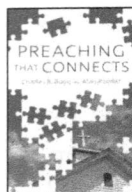

Preaching that Connects
Charles B. Bugg and Alan Redditt

How does the minister stay focused on the holy when the daily demands of the church seem relentless? How do we come to a preaching event with a sense that God is working in us and through us? In *Preaching that Connects*, Charles Bugg and Alan Redditt explore the balancing act of a minister's authority as preacher, sharing what the congregation needs to hear, and the communal role as pastor, listening to God alongside congregants.

978-157312-887-2 128 pages/pb **$15.00**

Reading Isaiah
(Reading the Old Testament series)
A Literary and Theological Commentary
Hyun Chul Paul Kim

While closely exegeting key issues of each chapter, this commentary also explores interpretive relevance and significance between ancient texts and the modern world. Engaging with theological messages of the book of Isaiah as a unified whole, the commentary will both illuminate and inspire readers to wrestle with its theological implications for today's church and society.

978-1-57312-925-1 352 pages/pb **$33.00**

Reading Jeremiah
(Reading the Old Testament series)
A Literary and Theological Commentary
Corrine Carvalho

Reflecting the ways that communal tragedy permeates communal identity, the book of Jeremiah as literary text embodies the confusion, disorientation, and search for meaning that all such tragedy elicits. Just as the fall of Jerusalem fractured the Judean community and undercut every foundation on which it built its identity, so too the book itself (or more properly, the scroll) jumbles images, genres, and perspectives.

978-1-57312-924-4 186 pages/pb **$32.00**

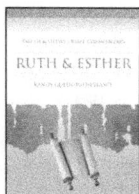

Ruth & Esther (Smyth & Helwys Bible Commentary)
Kandy Queen-Sutherland

Ruth and Esther are the only two women for whom books of the Hebrew Bible are named. This distinction in itself sets the books apart from other biblical texts that bear male names, address the community through its male members, recall the workings of God and human history through a predominately male perspective, and look to the future through male heirs. These books are particularly stories of survival. The story of Ruth focuses on the survival of a family; Esther focuses on the survival of a people.

978-1-57312-891-9 544 pages/hc **$60.00**

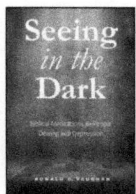

Seeing in the Dark
Biblical Meditations for People Dealing with Depression
Ronald D. Vaughan

This collection of biblical meditations is designed to be used as a daily devotional resource. Along with each meditation is a prayer based on that chapter's life lesson and a truth to affirm, a short summary to help readers remember what they've learned.

978-1-57312-973-2 144 pages/pb **$18.00**

Seeing the Son on the Way to the Moon
A NASA Engineer's Reflection on Science and Faith

W. Merlin Merritt

W. Merlin Merritt recounts his experiences during the early NASA space program and describes his struggle to integrate faith and science. He ultimately concludes that technology can point us to the grandeur of God's universe. The immensity and wonders of the cosmos point not only to an intelligent creator God but also to One who is actively involved in the universe. *978-1-57312-942-8 130 pages/pb* **$14.00**

Sessions with Isaiah (Sessions Bible Studies series)
What to Do When the World Caves In

James M. King

The book of Isaiah begins in the years of national stress when, under various kings, Israel was surrounded by more powerful neighbors and foolishly sought foreign alliances rather than dependence on Yahweh. It continues with the natural result of that unfaithfulness: conquest by the great power in the region, Babylon, and the captivity of many of Israel's best and brightest in that foreign land. The book concludes anticipating their return to the land of promise and strong admonitions about the people's conduct—but we also hear God's reassuring messages of comfort and restoration, offered to all who repent. *978-1-57312-942-8 130 pages/pb* **$14.00**

Stained-Glass Millennials

Rob Lee

We've heard the narrative that millennials are done with the institutional church; they've packed up and left. This book is an alternative to that story and chronicles the journey of millennials who are investing their lives in the institution because they believe in the church's resurrecting power. Through anecdotes and interviews, Rob Lee takes readers on a journey toward God's unfolding future for the church, a beloved institution in desperate need of change. *978-1-57312-926-8 156 pages/pb* **$16.00**

Star Thrower
A Pastor's Handbook

William Powell Tuck

In *Star Thrower: A Pastor's Handbook*, William Powell Tuck draws on over fifty years of experience to share his perspective on being an effective pastor. He describes techniques for sermon preparation, pastoral care, and church administration, as well as for conducting Communion, funeral, wedding, and baptismal services. He also includes advice for working with laity and church staff, coping with church conflict, and nurturing one's own spiritual and family life. *978-1-57312-889-6 244 pages/pb* **$15.00**

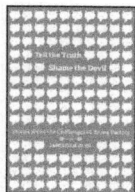

Tell the Truth, Shame the Devil
Stories about the Challenges of Young Pastors
James Elllis III, ed.

A pastor's life is uniquely difficult. *Tell the Truth, Shame the Devil*, then, is an attempt to expose some of the challenges that young clergy often face. While not exhaustive, this collection of essays is a superbly compelling and diverse introduction to how tough being a pastor under the age of thirty-five can be. *978-1-57312-839-1 198 pages/pb* **$18.00**

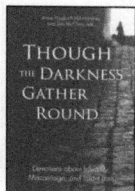

Though the Darkness Gather Round
Devotions about Infertility, Miscarriage, and Infant Loss
Mary Elizabeth Hill Hanchey and Erin McClain, eds.

Much courage is required to weather the long grief of infertility and the sudden grief of miscarriage and infant loss. This collection of devotions by men and women, ministers, chaplains, and lay leaders who can speak of such sorrow, is a much-needed resource and precious gift for families on this journey and the faith communities that walk beside them.

978-1-57312-811-7 180 pages/pb **$19.00**

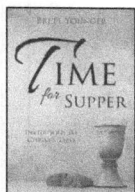

Time for Supper
Invitations to Christ's Table
Brett Younger

Some scholars suggest that every meal in literature is a communion scene. Could every meal in the Bible be a communion text? Could every passage be an invitation to God's grace? These meditations on the Lord's Supper help us listen to the myriad of ways God invites us to gratefully, reverently, and joyfully share the cup of Christ. *978-1-57312-720-2 246 pages/pb* **$18.00**

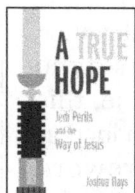

A True Hope
Jedi Perils and the Way of Jesus
Joshua Hays

Star Wars offers an accessible starting point for considering substantive issues of faith, philosophy, and ethics. In *A True Hope*, Joshua Hays explores some of these challenging ideas through the sayings of the Jedi Masters, examining the ways the worldview of the Jedi is at odds with that of the Bible. *978-1-57312-770-7 186 pages/pb* **$18.00**

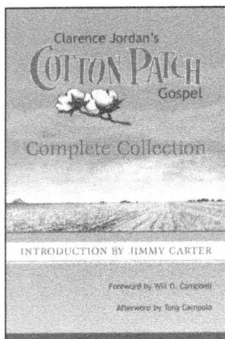

www.ingramcontent.com/pod-product-compliance
Lightning Source LLC
Chambersburg PA
CBHW071344090426
42738CB00012B/3000